Best Garden Plants *for* New England

Thomas Mickey • *Alison Beck*

Lone Pine Publishing International

The Distributor: Lone Pine Publishing
1808 B Street NW, Suite 140
Auburn, WA, USA 98001
Website: www.lonepinepublishing.com

Library and Archives Canada Cataloguing in Publication

Mickey, Thomas J.
    Best garden plants for New England / Thomas Mickey, Alison Beck.

Includes index.
ISBN-13: 978–976–8200–11–2
ISBN-10: 976–8200–11–1

    1. Plants, Ornamental—New England. 2. Gardening—New England.
I. Beck, Alison, 1971– II. Title.

SB453.2.N3M53 2006   635.9'0974   C2005–907061–7

Scanning & Electronic Film: Elite Lithographers Co.

Front cover photographs by Tamara Eder and Tim Matheson except where noted. *Clockwise from top right:* floribunda rose 'Iceberg,' crabapple blossom, iris, lilac leaves, daylily, sweet potato vine, daylily, lily, columbine, lily (Erika Flatt)

Photography: All photography by Tim Matheson and Tamara Eder except:
David Cavagnaro 159a; Janet Davis 91b; Therese D'Monte 159b; Don Doucette 122b; Derek Fell 1, 4, 45b, 91a, 108a, 143a, 157a; Erika Flatt 10a, 66b, 105a, 152b, 156a; Anne Gordon 82; Lynne Harrison 117a&b; Horticolor 141b; Duncan Kelbaugh 152a; Liz Klose 74a, 76a&b; Dawn Loewen 75a, 87a; Janet Loughrey 157b; Kim O'Leary 13a, 85a, 107a, 151a, 154a, 165b; Allison Penko 8b, 37a, 51a, 54, 58a, 61a, 63a, 65b, 74b, 87b, 88a, 97a 100a, 104b, 106a, 107b, 112b, 115a&b, 118a&b, 121b, 140b, 145b, 150b, 151b, 155a; Laura Peters 9a&b, 10b, 19a, 28a, 38a, 48b, 51b, 52a&b, 61b, 65a, 66a, 71a&b, 78a&b, 89a 102a&b, 123, 124a, 135a&b, 138a, 144a, 145a, 146a, 147a&b, 148a&b, 156b, 160a&b, 161b, 162a&b, 163a&b, 166a&b, 167a&b, 168a&b; Photos.com 158a; Poulsen Roser ApS 128a&b; Robert Ritchie 43b, 47a, 50a&b, 111a, 127a, 134a, 136a, 165a; Gene Sasse-Weeks Roses 131; Leila Sidi 158b; Joy Spurr 141a; Peter Thompstone 18a, 53a, 55a, 64a&b, 69a; Mark Turner 94a; Don Williamson 144b, 153a&b, 161a; Tim Wood 120a, 122a.

PC: P13

Table of Contents

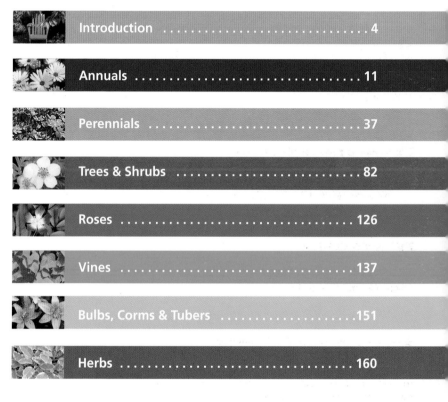

Introduction

Starting a garden can seem like a daunting task, but it is also an exciting and rewarding adventure. With so many plants to choose from, the challenge is deciding which ones and how many of each you can include in your garden. This book is intended to give beginning gardeners the information they need to start planning and planting gardens of their own. It describes a wide variety of plants and provides basic descriptions of plants, planting and growing information and tips for getting you started producing a beautiful and functional landscape.

The New England summer growing season is quite short. The winters can be cold but ensure a good period of dormancy and plenty of flowers in spring. Rainfall is fairly predictable and the soil, though not without its challenges, supports a variety of healthy plants.

Hardiness zones and frost dates are two terms often used when discussing climate and gardening. Hardiness zones are based on the minimum possible winter temperatures. Plants are rated based on the zones in which they grow successfully. The last-frost date in spring combined with the first-frost date in fall allows us to predict the length of the growing season and gives us an idea of when we can begin planting out.

Microclimates are small areas that are generally warmer or colder than the surrounding area. Buildings, fences, trees and other large structures can provide extra shelter in winter but may trap heat in summer, thus creating a warmer microclimate. The bottoms of hills are usually colder than the tops but may not be as windy. Take advantage of these areas when you plan your garden and choose your plants; you may even grow out-of-zone plants successfully in a warm, sheltered location.

Getting Started

When planning your garden, start with a quick analysis of the garden as it is now. Plants have different requirements and it is best to put the right plant in the right place rather than to try to change your garden to suit the plants you want.

Knowing which parts of your garden receive the most and least amounts of sunlight will help you choose the proper plants and decide where to plant them. Light is classified into four basic groups: full sun (direct, unobstructed light all or most of the day); partial shade (direct sun for about half the day and shade for the rest); light shade (shade all or most of the day with some sun filtering through to

ground level); and full shade (no direct sunlight). Most plants prefer a certain amount of light, but many can adapt to a range of light levels.

The soil is the foundation of a good garden. Plants use the soil to hold themselves upright but also rely on the many resources it holds: air, water, nutrients, organic matter and a host of microbes. The particle size of the soil influences the amount of air, water and nutrients it can hold. Sand, with the largest particles, has a lot of air space and allows water and nutrients to drain quickly. Clay, with the smallest particles, is high in nutrients but has very little air space. Water is therefore slow to penetrate clay and slow to drain from it.

Soil acidity or alkalinity (measured on the pH scale) influences the amount and type of nutrients available to plants. A pH of 7 is neutral; a lower pH is more acidic. Most plants prefer

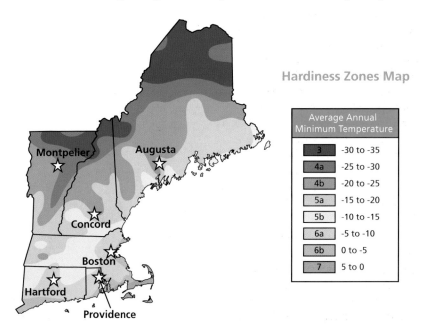

Hardiness Zones Map

Average Annual Minimum Temperature	
3	-30 to -35
4a	-25 to -30
4b	-20 to -25
5a	-15 to -20
5b	-10 to -15
6a	-5 to -10
6b	0 to -5
7	5 to 0

a soil with a pH of 5.5–7.5. Soil-testing kits are available at most garden centers, and soil samples can be sent to testing facilities for a more thorough analysis. This will give you an idea of what plants will do well in your soil and what soil amendments may be needed.

Compost is one of the best and most important amendments you can add to any type of soil. Compost improves soil by adding organic matter and nutrients, introducing soil microbes, increasing water retention and improving drainage. Compost can be purchased or you can make it in your own backyard.

Selecting Plants

It's important to purchase healthy plants that are free of pests and diseases. Such plants will establish quickly in your garden and won't introduce problems that may spread to other plants. You should have a good idea of what the plant is supposed to look like at maturity—the color and shape of the leaves and the habit of the plant—and then inspect the plant for signs of disease or insect damage.

Many plants are container-grown. This is an efficient way for nurseries and greenhouses to grow plants, but when plants grow in a restricted space for too long, they can become pot bound with their roots densely encircling the inside of the pot. Avoid purchasing plants in this condition; they are often stressed and can take longer to establish. It is often possible to remove pots temporarily to look at the condition of the roots. You can check for soil-borne insects, rotten roots and girdling or pot-bound roots at the same time. Roots wrapping densely around the inside of a pot must be lightly pruned or teased apart before planting.

Planting Basics

The following tips apply to all plants.

• Prepare the garden before planting. Remove weeds, make any needed amendments and dig or till the soil in preparation for planting if you are starting a new landscape. This may be more difficult in established beds to which you want to add a single plant. The prepared area should be the size of the plant's mature root system.

• Settle the soil with water. Good contact between the roots and the soil is important, but if you press the soil down too firmly, as often happens when you step on it, you can cause compaction, which reduces the movement of water through the soil and leaves very few air spaces. Instead, pour water in as you fill the hole with soil. The water will settle the soil evenly without allowing it to compact.

Gently remove container.

Ensure proper planting depth.

Backfill with soil.

- Unwrap the roots. It is always best to remove any container before planting to give roots the chance to spread out naturally when planted. In particular, you should remove plastic containers, fiber pots, wire and burlap before planting trees. Fiber pots decompose very slowly, if at all, and draw moisture away from the plant. Burlap may be synthetic, which won't decompose, and wire can eventually strangle the roots as they mature. The only exceptions to this rule are the peat pots and pellets used to start annuals and vegetables; these decompose and can be planted with the young transplants. Even these peat pots should be sliced down the sides and any of the pot that will be exposed above ground removed to prevent water from being drawn away from the roots.

- Accommodate the rootball. If you prepared your planting spot ahead of time so it will accommodate the mature roots, your planting hole will only need to be big enough to accommodate the rootball with the roots spread out slightly.

- Know the mature size. Plant based on how big plants will grow rather than how big they are when you plant them. Large plants should have enough room to mature without interfering with walls, roof overhangs, power lines, walkways and surrounding plants.

- Plant at the same depth. Plants generally like to grow at a specific level in relation to the soil and should be planted at the same level they were at in the pot or container before you transplanted them.

- Identify your plants. Keep track of what's what in your garden by putting a tag next to each plant when you plant it. A gardening journal is a great place to list the plants you have and where you planted them. It is very easy for beginning and seasoned gardeners alike to forget exactly what they planted and where they planted it.

- Water deeply. It's better to water deeply once every week or two, depending on the plant, rather than to water lightly more often. Deep and thorough watering forces roots to grow as they search for water and helps them survive dry spells when water bans may restrict your watering regime. Always check the rootzone before you water as some soils hold more water for longer than other soils. More gardeners overwater than underwater. Mulching helps retain moisture and reduces watering needs. Containers are the watering exception as they can quickly dry out and may even need watering every day.

Settle backfilled soil with water.

Water the plant well.

Add a layer of mulch.

Choosing Plants

When choosing plants, you want to aim for a variety of sizes, shapes, textures, features and bloom times. Features like decorative fruit, variegated or colorful leaves and interesting bark provide interest when plants aren't blooming. This way you will have a garden that captivates your attention all year.

Annuals

Annuals are planted new each year and are only expected to last for a single growing season. Their flowers and decorative foliage provide bright splashes of color and can fill in spaces around immature trees, shrubs and perennials.

Annuals are easy to plant and are often sold in small cell-packs of four or six. The roots quickly fill the space in these small packs, so the small rootball should be broken up before planting. Split the ball in two up the center, or run your thumb up each side to break up the roots.

Many annuals are grown from seed and can be started directly in the garden once the soil begins to warm up.

Perennials

Perennials grow for three or more years. They usually die back to the

Trees and shrubs provide backbone to the mixed border.

ground each fall and send up new shoots in spring, though they can also be evergreen or semi-shrubby. They often have a shorter period of bloom than annuals but require less care.

Many perennials benefit from being divided every few years, usually in early spring while the plants are still dormant or, in some cases, after flowering. This keeps them growing and blooming vigorously, and in some cases controls their spread. Dividing involves digging the plant up, removing dead debris, breaking the plant into several pieces using a sharp knife, spade or saw and replanting some or all of the pieces. Extra pieces can be shared with family, friends and neighbors.

Trees & Shrubs

Trees and shrubs provide the bones of the garden. They are often the slowest growing plants but usually live the longest. Characterized by leaf type, they may be deciduous or evergreen, and broad-leaved or needled.

Trees should have as little disturbed soil as possible at the bottom of the

Perennials add color to the border year after year.

Roses are lovely on their own or in mixed borders.

Training vines to climb arbors adds structure to the garden.

planting hole. Loose dirt settles over time and sinking even an inch can kill some trees. The prepared area for trees and shrubs needs to be at least two to four times bigger than the rootball.

Staking, sometimes recommended for newly planted trees, is only necessary for trees over 5' tall. Stakes support the rootball until it grows enough to support the tree. Stakes should allow the trunk to move with the wind.

Pruning is more often required for shrubs than trees. It helps them maintain an attractive shape and can improve blooming.

Roses

Roses are beautiful shrubs with lovely, often-fragrant blooms. Traditionally, most roses only bloomed once in the growing season, but new varieties bloom all, or almost all, summer. Repeat blooming, or recurrent, roses should be deadheaded to encourage more flower production. One-time bloomers should be left for the colorful hips that develop.

Generally, roses prefer a fertile, well-prepared planting area. A rule of thumb is to prepare an area 24" across, front to back and side to side, and 24" deep. Add plenty of compost or other fertile organic matter, and keep roses well watered during the growing season. Many roses are quite durable and will adapt to poorer conditions. Grafted roses should be planted with the graft two inches below the soil line. When watering, avoid getting water on the foliage to reduce the spread of blackspot.

Vines

Vines or climbing plants are useful for screening and shade, especially in a location too small for a tree. They may be woody or herbaceous, and annual or perennial. Vines may physically cling to surfaces, may have wrapping tendrils or stems or may need to be tied in place with string.

Sturdy trellises, arbors, porch railings, fences, walls, poles and trees are all possible vine supports. If a support is needed, ensure it's in place before you plant to avoid disturbing the roots

Crocuses herald the arrival of spring.

later. Choose a support that is suitable for the vine you are growing. It needs to be sturdy enough to hold the plant up and should match the growing habit—clinging, wrapping or tied—of the vine.

Bulbs, Corms & Tubers

These plants have fleshy underground storage organs that allow them to survive extended periods of dormancy. They are often grown for the bright

Many herbs grow well in pots.

splashes of color their flowers provide. They may be spring, summer or fall flowering. Each has an ideal depth and time of year at which it should be planted.

Hardy bulbs can be left in the ground and will flower every year. Some popular tender plants are grown from bulbs, corms or tubers and are generally lifted from the garden in late summer or fall as the foliage dies back. These are stored in a cool, frost-free location for winter, to be replanted in spring.

Herbs

Herbs are plants with medicinal, culinary or other economic purposes. A few common culinary herbs are included in this book. Even if you don't cook with them, the often-fragrant foliage adds its aroma to the garden, and the plants can be quite decorative in form, leaf and flower. A conveniently placed container—perhaps near the kitchen door—of your favorite herbs will yield plenty of flavor and fragrance all summer.

Many herbs have pollen-producing flowers that attract butterflies, bees, hummingbirds and predatory insects to your garden. Predatory insects feast on problem insects such as aphids, mealy bugs and whiteflies.

A Final Comment

The more you discover about the fascinating world of plants, whether it be from reading books, talking to other gardeners, appreciating the creative designs of others, or experimenting with something new in your own garden, the more rewarding your gardening experience will be. This book is intended as a guide to germinate and grow your passion for plants.

Angelonia
Angelonia

A. angustifolia 'Alba' (above), *A. angustifolia* 'Blue Pacific' (below)

With its loose, airy spikes of orchid-like flowers, angelonia makes a welcome addition to the garden.

Growing

Angelonia prefers **full sun** but tolerates a bit of shade. The soil should be **fertile, moist** and **well drained**. Although this plant grows naturally in damp areas, such as along ditches and near ponds, it is fairly drought tolerant. Plant out after the chance of frost has passed.

Tips

Angelonia makes a good addition to an annual or mixed border where it is most attractive when planted in groups. It is also suited to a pondside or streamside planting.

Recommended

A. angustifolia is a bushy, upright plant with loose spikes of flowers in varied shades of purple. Cultivars with white or bicolored flowers are available.

The individual flowers look a bit like orchid blossoms, but angelonia is actually in the same family as snapdragon.

Also called: angel wings, summer snapdragon
Features: attractive, purple, blue, white, bicolored flowers **Height:** 12–24"
Spread: 12"

Bacopa
Sutera

S. *cordata* (above & below)

Bacopa is a perennial that is grown as an annual outdoors. It will thrive as a houseplant in a bright room.

Bacopa snuggles under and around the stems of taller plants, forming a dense carpet dotted with tiny, white to pale lavender flowers, and eventually drifts over pot edges to form a waterfall of stars.

Growing
Bacopa grows well in **partial shade**, with protection from the hot afternoon sun. The soil should be of **average fertility, humus rich, moist** and **well drained**. Don't allow this plant to dry out, or the leaves will quickly die. Cutting back dead growth may encourage new shoots to form.

Tips
Bacopa is a popular plant for hanging baskets, mixed containers and window boxes. It is not recommended as a bedding plant because it fizzles quickly when the weather gets hot, particularly if you forget to water. Plant it where you will see it every day so you will remember to water it.

Recommended
S. cordata is a compact, trailing plant that bears small, white flowers all summer. Cultivars with larger, white or lavender flowers, or gold and green variegated foliage are available.

Features: decorative, white or lavender flowers; foliage; habit **Height:** 3–6"
Spread: 12–20"

Begonia
Begonia

With its beautiful flowers, compact habit and decorative foliage, there is sure to be a begonia to meet your shade gardening needs.

Growing
Light or partial shade is best, though some wax begonias tolerate sun if their soil is kept moist. The soil should be **fertile, rich in organic matter** and **well drained** with a **neutral or acidic pH**. Allow the soil to dry out slightly between waterings, particularly for tuberous begonias. Begonias love warm weather, so don't plant them before the soil warms in spring. If they sit in cold soil, they may become stunted and fail to thrive.

Tips
All begonias are useful for shaded garden beds and planters. The trailing tuberous varieties can be used in hanging baskets and along rock walls where the flowers will cascade over the edges. Wax begonias have a neat, rounded habit that makes them particularly attractive as edging plants. Rex begonias, with their dramatic foliage, are useful as specimen plants in containers and beds.

Recommended
B. Rex Cultorum **Hybrids** (rex begonias) are grown for their dramatic, colorful foliage.

B. semperflorens (wax begonias) have pink, white, red or bicolored flowers, and green, bronze, reddish or white-variegated foliage.

B. semperflorens (above), *B. x tuberhybrida* (below)

B. **x** *tuberhybrida* (tuberous begonias) are generally sold as tubers and are popular for their flowers, which grow in many shades of red, pink, yellow, orange or white.

Features: pink, white, red, yellow, orange, bicolored, picotee flowers; decorative foliage
Height: 6–24" **Spread:** 6–24"

California Poppy
Eschscholzia

E. californica (above & below)

The petals of California poppy are edible. Their intense color will brighten up a salad.

California poppies are aptly described as the shimmering, fluttering apricot orange jewels of the West.

Growing

California poppy prefers **full sun**. The soil should be of **poor or average fertility** and **well drained**. With too rich a soil, the growth will be lush and green, but the plant will bear few, if any, flowers. This plant is drought tolerant once established, but it requires a lot of water for germination and until it begins flowering.

Never start this plant indoors because it dislikes having its roots disturbed. California poppy will sprout quickly when sown directly in the garden in early to mid-spring.

Tips

California poppy can be included in an annual border or annual planting in a cottage garden. This plant self-seeds wherever it is planted; it is perfect for naturalizing in a meadow or rock garden where it will come back year after year.

Recommended

E. californica forms a mound of delicate, feathery, blue-green foliage. It bears satiny, orange or yellow flowers all summer. Cultivars with semi-double or double flowers and flowers in red, cream or pink are available.

Features: orange, yellow, red, violet, cream, and less commonly pink, flowers; attractive feathery foliage **Height:** 8–18"
Spread: 8–18"

Cleome
Cleome

C. *hassleriana* Royal Queen Series (above), C. *hassleriana* (below)

Create a bold and exotic display in your garden with these lovely and unusual flowers.

Growing

Cleome prefers **full sun** but tolerates **partial shade**. Plants **adapt to most soils**, though mixing in organic matter to help retain water is a good idea. These plants are drought-tolerant but perform best when watered regularly. Pinch out the tip of the center stem on young plants to encourage branching and more blooms. Deadhead to prolong blooming and to reduce prolific self-seeding.

Tips

Cleome can be planted in groups at the back of a border or in the center of an island bed. These striking plants also make an attractive addition to a large mixed container planting.

Recommended

C. hassleriana is a tall, upright plant with strong, supple, thorny stems. The foliage and flowers of this plant have a strong but not unpleasant scent. Flowers are borne in loose, rounded clusters at the ends of the leafy stems. Many cultivars are available.

C. serrulata (Rocky Mountain bee plant) is native to western North America but is rarely available commercially. The thornless dwarf cultivar **'Solo'** is regularly available to be grown from seed and grows 12–18" tall with pink and white flowers.

Also called: spider flower **Features:** large, airy, purple, pink, white flowers; attractive, scented foliage; thorny stems **Height:** 1–5' **Spread:** 12–24"

Coleus
Solenostemon (Coleus)

S. *scutellarioides* cultivars (above & below)

From brash yellows, oranges and reds to rosy pinks, deep maroons and almost black selections, the colors, textures and variations of coleus are almost limitless.

Growing
Depending on the cultivar, coleus prefers **light or partial shade** but tolerates full shade if not too dense, or full sun if the plants are watered regularly. The soil should be of **rich to average fertility, humus rich, moist** and **well drained**.

Refrigerate the seeds for one or two days before planting them on the soil surface; the cold temperature assists in breaking the seeds' dormancy. They need light to germinate. The seedlings are green at first, but leaf variegation develops as the plants mature.

Tips
The bold, colorful foliage makes coleus dramatic when the plants are grouped together as edging plants or in beds, borders and mixed containers. Coleus can also be grown indoors as a houseplant in a bright room.

It is best to pinch off the flower buds when they develop, because the plants tend to stretch out and become less attractive after they flower.

Recommended
S. scutellarioides (*Coleus blumei* var. *verschaffeltii*) forms a bushy mound of foliage. The leaf edges range from slightly toothed to very ruffled. The leaves are usually multi-colored, with shades ranging from pale greenish yellow to deep purple-black. Cultivars are available, but many cannot be started from seed.

Features: brightly colored foliage; insignificant, light purple flowers
Height: 6–36" **Spread:** 6–36"

Dusty Miller

Senecio

S. cineraria 'Cirrus' (above), *S. cineraria* (below)

Dusty miller makes an artful addition to planters, window boxes and mixed borders where the soft, silvery gray, deeply lobed foliage makes a good backdrop to show off the brightly colored flowers of other annuals.

Growing

Dusty miller prefers **full sun** but tolerates light shade. The soil should be of **average fertility** and **well drained**.

Tips

The soft, silvery, lacy leaves of this plant are its main feature. Dusty miller is used primarily as an edging plant, but is also attractive in beds, borders and containers. Pinch off the flowers before they bloom. They aren't showy and they steal energy that would otherwise go to producing more foliage.

Recommended

S. cineraria forms a mound of fuzzy, silvery gray, lobed or finely divided foliage. Many cultivars have been developed with impressive foliage colors and shapes.

Mix dusty miller with geraniums, begonias or celosias to complement the vibrant colors of these flowers.

Features: silvery foliage; neat habit; insignificant, yellow flowers **Height:** 12–24"
Spread: 10–24"

Fan Flower
Scaevola

S. aemula (above & below)

Fan flower's intriguing one-sided flowers add interest to hanging baskets, planters and window boxes.

Growing

Fan flower grows well in **full sun** or **light shade**. The soil should be of **average fertility, moist** and very **well drained**. Water regularly because this plant doesn't like to dry out completely. It does, however, recover quickly from wilting when watered.

Tips

Fan flower is popular for hanging baskets and containers, but it can also be used along the tops of rock walls and in rock gardens where it will trail down. This plant makes an interesting addition to mixed borders or it can be used under shrubs, where the long, trailing stems will form an attractive groundcover.

Recommended

S. aemula forms a mound of foliage from which trailing stems emerge. The fan-shaped flowers come in shades of purple, usually with white bases. The species is rarely grown because there are many improved cultivars.

Given the right conditions, this Australian plant will flower abundantly from April through to frost.

Features: unique, blue or purple flowers; trailing habit **Height:** up to 8"
Spread: 36" or more

Geranium
Pelargonium

Tough, predictable, sun-loving and drought resistant, geraniums have earned their place as flowering favorites in the annual garden. If you are looking for something out of the ordinary, seek out the scented geraniums with their fragrant and often-decorative foliage.

Growing
Geraniums prefer **full sun** but tolerate partial shade, though they may not bloom as profusely. The soil should be **fertile** and **well drained**. Deadheading is essential to keep geraniums blooming and looking neat.

Tips
Geraniums are very popular annual plants, used in borders, beds, planters, hanging baskets and window boxes.

Geraniums are perennials that are treated as annuals and can be kept indoors over winter in a bright room.

Recommended
P. peltatum (ivy-leaved geranium) has thick, waxy leaves and a trailing habit. Many cultivars are available.

P. **species** and **cultivars** (scented geraniums, scented pelargoniums) is a large group of geraniums that have fragrant leaves. The scents are grouped into categories such as rose, mint, citrus, fruit, spice and pungent.

P. zonale (zonal geranium) is a bushy plant with red, pink, purple, orange or white flowers and, frequently, banded or multi-colored foliage. Many cultivars are available.

Features: red, pink, violet, orange, salmon, white, purple flowers; decorative or scented foliage; variable habits **Height:** 8–24"
Spread: 6"–4'

P. zonale Fireworks Collection (above)
P. peltatum (below)

Ivy-leaved geranium is one of the most beautiful plants to include in a mixed hanging basket.

Impatiens
Impatiens

I. walleriana (above), *I. hawkeri* (below)

The English named I. walleriana *busy Lizzie because it flowers continuously through the growing season.*

Impatiens are the high-wattage darlings of the shade garden, delivering masses of flowers in a wide variety of colors.

Growing

Impatiens do best in **partial shade** or **light shade** but tolerate full shade or, if kept moist, full sun. New Guinea impatiens are the best adapted to sunny locations. The soil should be **fertile, humus rich, moist** and **well drained**.

Tips

Impatiens are known for their ability to grow and flower profusely, even in shade. Mass plant them in beds under trees, along shady fences or walls or in porch planters. They also look lovely in hanging baskets. New Guinea impatiens are grown as much for their variegated leaves as for their flowers.

Recommended

I. hawkeri (New Guinea Hybrids; New Guinea impatiens) flowers in shades of red, orange, pink, purple or white. The foliage is often variegated with a yellow stripe down the center of each leaf.

I. walleriana (impatiens, busy Lizzie) flowers in shades of purple, red, burgundy, pink, yellow, salmon, orange, apricot, white or can be bicolored. Dozens of cultivars are available.

Also called: busy Lizzie **Features:** flowers in shades of purple, red, burgundy, pink, yellow, salmon, orange, apricot, white, bicolored; grows well in shade **Height:** 6–36" **Spread:** 12–24"

Licorice Plant

Helichrysum

H. petiolare 'Silver' (above), H. petiolare 'Limelight' (below)

The silvery sheen of licorice plant is caused by a fine, soft pubescence on the leaves. It is a perfect complement to any plant because silver is the ultimate blending color.

Growing

Licorice plant prefers **full sun**. The soil should be of **poor to average fertility, neutral or alkaline** and **well drained**. Licorice plant wilts when the soil dries but revives quickly once watered. If it outgrows its space, snip it back with a pair of pruners, shears or even scissors.

Tips

Prized for its foliage rather than its flowers, licorice plant is a perennial grown as an annual. Include it in your hanging baskets, planters and window boxes to provide a soft, silvery backdrop for the colorful flowers of other plants.

Licorice plant can also be used as a groundcover in beds, borders, rock gardens and along the tops of retaining walls.

Recommended

H. petiolare is a trailing plant with fuzzy, gray-green leaves. Cultivars are more common than the species and include varieties with lime green, silver or variegated leaves.

Licorice plant is a good indicator plant for hanging baskets. When you see licorice plant wilting, it is time to water your baskets.

Features: trailing habit; colorful, fuzzy foliage
Height: 20" **Spread:** about 36"; sometimes up to 6'

Lobelia

Lobelia

L. erinus 'Sapphire' (above), *L. erinus* cultivars (below)

Delicate and airy in appearance, lobelia still manages to add a bright splash of color to the garden.

Growing

Lobelia will grow well in **full sun, partial shade** or **light shade**. The soil should be **fertile, humus rich, moist** and **well drained**. Sun early rather than late in the day is best, and plants will need to be kept well watered in sunny locations. Lobelia grows best when nights are cool and may fade during hot summer weather.

Tips

Use lobelia along the edges of beds and borders, on rock walls, in rock gardens, in mixed containers and in hanging baskets.

Recommended

L. erinus plants may be rounded and bushy, or low and trailing. It bears flowers in shades of blue, purple, red, pink or white. There are many cultivars available, including some newer selections that are better able to tolerate hot weather.

Trim plants back when they begin to fade in the summer and keep them well watered. They will revive when the weather cools in late summer and fall.

Features: blue, purple, red, pink, white flowers; airy habit **Height:** 4–10"
Spread: 4–10"

Love-in-a-Mist
Nigella

N. damascena (above & below)

*L*ove-in-a-mist's ferny foliage and delicate, blue flowers blend with most plants. It has a tendency to self-sow and may show up in unexpected spots in your garden for years to come.

Growing

Love-in-a-mist prefers **full sun**. The soil should be of **average fertility, light** and **well drained**.

Direct sow seeds at two-week intervals all spring to prolong the blooming period.

Tips

This attractive, airy plant is often used in mixed beds and borders. The flowers appear to float above the delicate foliage. The blooming may be slow, and the plants may die back if the weather gets too hot in summer.

The stems of this plant can be a bit floppy and may benefit from being staked with twiggy branches. Poke branches into the dirt around the plant when it is young, and the plant will grow up between the twigs.

Recommended

N. damascena forms a loose mound of finely divided foliage. Cultivars are available with a wider variety of flower colors than the blue offered by the species.

The aromatic seeds have been used as a cooking spice and as medicine.

Also called: devil-in-a-bush
Features: feathery foliage; exotic, blue, white, pink, purple flowers **Height:** 16–24"
Spread: 8–12"

Marigold
Tagetes

T. tenuifolia (above), *T. patula* hybrid (below)

Marigolds are often included in vegetable gardens for their reputed insect- and nematode-repelling qualities.

From the large, exotic, ruffled flowers of African marigold to the tiny flowers on the low-growing signet marigold, the warm colors and fresh scent of marigolds add a festive touch to the garden.

Growing
Marigolds grow best in **full sun**. The soil should be of **average fertility** and **well drained**. These plants are drought tolerant and hold up well in windy, rainy weather. Sow seed directly in the garden after the chance of frost has passed. Deadhead to prolong blooming and to keep plants tidy.

Tips
Mass planted or mixed with other plants, marigolds make a vibrant addition to beds, borders and container gardens. These plants will thrive in the hottest, driest parts of your garden.

Recommended
There are many cultivars available for all the species. *T. erecta* (African marigold, American marigold, Aztec marigold) are the largest plants with the biggest flowers. *T. patula* (French marigold) is low growing and has a wide range of flower colors. *T. tenuifolia* (signet marigold) has become more popular recently because of its feathery foliage and small, dainty flowers. *T.* **Triploid Hybrids** (triploid marigold) have been developed by crossing French and African marigolds, which results in plants with huge flowers and compact growth.

Features: yellow, red, orange, brown, gold, cream, bicolored flowers; fragrant foliage
Height: 6–36" **Spread:** 12–24"

Million Bells
Calibrachoa

Million bells is charming, and given the right conditions, blooms continuously during the growing season.

Growing
Million bells prefers **full sun**. The soil should be **fertile, moist** and **well drained**. Although it prefers to be watered regularly, million bells is fairly drought resistant once established. It becomes hardier over summer and as the weather cools, blooming well into autumn.

Tips
Popular for planters and hanging baskets, million bells is also attractive in beds and borders. It grows all summer and needs plenty of room to spread or it will overtake other flowers. Pinch back to keep plants compact.

C. 'Terracotta' (above)
C. 'Trailing Pink' and 'Trailing Blue' (below)

Recommended
Calibrachoa **hybrids** have a dense, trailing habit. They bear small flowers that look like petunias, and cultivars are available in a wide range of flower colors.

Calibrachoa flowers close at night and on cloudy days.

Also called: calibrachoa, trailing petunia
Features: pink, purple, yellow, red-orange, white, blue flowers; trailing habit
Height: 6–12" **Spread:** up to 24"

Nasturtium

Tropaeolum

T. majus (above), *T. majus* 'Alaska' (below)

The leaves and flowers are edible, adding a peppery flavor to salads.

These fast-growing, brightly colored flowers are easy to grow, making them popular with beginners and experienced gardeners alike.

Growing

Nasturtiums prefer **full sun** but tolerate some shade. The soil should be of **poor to average fertility, light, moist** and **well drained**. Soil that is too rich or has too much nitrogen fertilizer will result in lots of leaves and very few flowers. Let the soil drain completely between waterings. Sow directly in the garden once the danger of frost has passed.

Tips

Nasturtiums are used in beds, borders, containers and hanging baskets and on sloped banks. The climbing varieties are grown up trellises or over rock walls or places that need concealing. These plants thrive in poor locations, and they make an interesting addition to plantings on hard-to-mow slopes.

Recommended

T. majus has a trailing habit, but many of the cultivars have bushier, more refined habits. Cultivars offer differing flower colors or variegated foliage.

Features: red, orange, yellow, burgundy, pink, cream, gold, white, bicolored flowers; attractive foliage; edible leaves and flowers; varied habits **Height:** 12–18" for dwarf varieties; up to 10' for trailing varieties **Spread:** equal to height

Nicotiana
Nicotiana

Nicotianas were originally cultivated for the wonderful fragrance of the flowers. Although this feature, in some cases, has been lost in favor of an expanded selection of flower colors, fragrant varieties are still available.

Growing
Nicotianas grow equally well in **full sun, light shade** or **partial shade**. The soil should be **fertile, high in organic matter, moist** and **well drained**.

Tips
Nicotianas are popular in beds and borders. The dwarf varieties do well in containers.

Do not plant nicotianas near tomatoes because, as members of the same plant family, they share a vulnerability to many of the same diseases. Nicotiana plants may attract and harbor diseases that will hardly affect them but can kill tomatoes.

N. x sanderae Nicki Series (above & below)

Recommended
N. x *sanderae* (*N. alata* x *N. forgetiana*) is a hybrid from which many brightly colored and dwarf cultivars have been developed.

N. sylvestris grows up to 4' tall and bears white blooms that are fragrant in the evening.

The seeds require light to germinate, so if you start plants from seed, press them into the soil surface but don't cover them.

Also called: flowering tobacco plant
Features: fragrant or colorful, red, pink, green, yellow, white, purple flowers
Height: 1–5' **Spread:** 12"

Osteospurmum
Osteospurmum

O. 'Lemon Symphony' (above), *O. ecklonis* (below)

You may find these plants listed as both Osteospurmum *and* Dimorphotheca. *The latter is a closely related genus that used to include the species now listed as* Osteospurmum.

Because of osteospurmum's dislike of hot weather, it may be best to use these attractive daisies to add a bright splash of color in late summer and fall.

Growing
Osteospurmum grows best in **full sun**. The soil should be of **average fertility, moist** and **well drained**. Don't let plants dry out enough to wilt, but avoid over-watering as well. An organic mulch will keep the soil moist and reduce the need for watering. Deadhead to prolong blooming and to keep plants looking neat. Pinch young plants to encourage bushy growth.

Tips
Osteospurmum makes a bright addition to mixed containers and can be included in beds and borders. Late summer plantings will flower until the first heavy frost.

Recommended
O. ecklonis is a subshrub with a variable habit, ranging from quite upright in form to a more prostrate habit. Cultivars in the **Symphony Series** and **Soprano Series** are noted for their improved heat tolerance.

Also called: African daisy, Cape daisy
Features: attractive flowers in shades of orange, peach, yellow, pink, purple, lavender, white; often with contrasting, dark blue or purple centers **Height:** 10–20"
Spread: 10–20"

Pansy
Viola

V. x wittrockiana (above & below)

Colorful and cheerful, pansy flowers are a welcome sight in spring after a long, dreary winter.

Growing
Pansies prefer **full sun** but tolerate partial shade. The soil should be **fertile, moist** and **well drained**. Pansies do best when the weather is cool and may die back over the summer. They may rejuvenate in late summer, but it is often easier to pull up faded plants and replace them with new ones in fall. These may very well survive the winter and provide you with flowers again in spring.

Tips
Pansies can be used in beds and borders, and they are popular for mixing in with spring-flowering bulbs and primroses. They can also be grown in containers.

Recommended
V. **x *wittrockiana*** is a small bushy plant that bear flowers in a wide range of bright and pastel colors, often with markings near the centers of the petals that give the flowers a face-like appearance.

Pansy petals are edible and make delightful garnishes on salads and desserts.

Features: flowers in bright or pastel shades of blue, purple, red, orange, yellow, pink, white, often bicolored **Height:** 6–12" **Spread:** 6–12"

Petunia
Petunia

P. milliflora type 'Fantasy' (above), P. multiflora type (below)

For speedy growth, prolific bloom-ing and ease of care, petunias are hard to beat.

Growing

Petunias prefer **full sun**. The soil should be of **average to rich fertility, light, sandy** and **well drained**. Pinch halfway back in mid-summer to keep plants bushy and to encourage new growth and flowers.

Owing to the introduction of many new and exciting cultivars, petunias are once again among the most popular and sought after of the annual garden flowers.

Tips

Use petunias in beds, borders, containers and hanging baskets.

Recommended

P. x *hybrida* is a large group of popular, sun-loving annuals that fall into three categories: **grandifloras** have the largest flowers in the widest range of colors, but they can be damaged by rain; **multifloras** bear more flowers that are smaller and less easily damaged by heavy rain; and **millifloras** have the smallest flowers in the narrowest range of colors, but this type is the most prolific and least likely to be damaged by heavy rain.

Features: pink, purple, red, white, yellow, coral, blue, bicolored flowers; versatile plants
Height: 6–18" **Spread:** 12–24" or wider

Poppy
Papaver

Poppies seem to have been made to grow in groups. The many flowers swaying in a breeze, with their often-curving stems, seem to be having lively conversations with one another.

Growing
Poppies grow best in **full sun**. The soil should be **fertile** and **sandy** with lots of **organic matter** mixed in. **Good drainage** is essential. Direct sow every two weeks in spring. Mix the tiny seeds with fine sand for even sowing. Do not cover them, because the seeds need light for germination. Deadhead to prolong blooming.

Tips
Poppies work well in mixed borders where other plants are slow to fill in. Poppies will fill in empty spaces early in the season, then die back over the summer, leaving room for other plants. They can also be used in rock gardens, and the cut flowers are popular for fresh arrangements.

P. nudicaule (above & below)

Recommended
P. nudicaule (Iceland poppy) bears red, orange, yellow, pink or white flowers in spring and early summer.

P. rhoeas (Flanders poppy, Shirley poppy, field poppy, corn poppy) forms a basal rosette of foliage above which the flowers are borne on long stems in a wide range of colors.

P. somniferum (opium poppy) bears red, pink, white or purple, often showy, single or double flowers. Although propagation of the species is restricted in many countries because of its narcotic properties, several attractive and permitted cultivars have been developed for ornamental use.

Features: red, pink, white, purple, yellow, orange flowers **Height:** 2–4'
Spread: 12"

Salvia
Salvia

S. splendens (red) and *S. farinacea* (purple) with purple lobelia (above), *S. viridis* (below)

The salvias should be part of every annual garden. The attractive and varied forms have something to offer any garden style.

Growing

All salvia plants prefer **full sun** but tolerate light shade. The soil should be **moist** and **well drained** and of **average to rich fertility**, with lots of **organic matter**. To keep plants producing flowers, water often and fertilize monthly.

Tips

Salvias look good grouped in beds, borders and containers. The flowers are

There are over 900 species of Salvia.

long lasting and make good cut flowers for arrangements.

Recommended

S. argentea (silver sage) is grown for its large, fuzzy, silvery leaves. *S. coccinea* (Texas sage) is a bushy, upright plant that bears whorled spikes of white, pink, blue or purple flowers. *S. farinacea* (mealy cup sage, blue sage) has bright blue flowers clustered along stems powdered with silver. Cultivars are available. *S. splendens* (salvia, scarlet sage) is grown for its spikes of bright red, tubular flowers. Recently, cultivars have become available in white, pink, purple and orange. *S. viridis* (*S. horminium;* annual clary sage) is grown for its colorful pink, purple, blue or white bracts, rather than the tiny flowers within the bracts.

Also called: sage **Features:** red, blue, purple, burgundy, pink, orange, salmon, yellow, cream, white, bicolored, summer flowers; attractive foliage **Height:** 8"–4' **Spread:** 8"–4'

Snapdragon
Antirrhinum

Snapdragons are among the most appealing plants. The flower colors are always rich and vibrant, and even the most jaded gardeners are tempted to squeeze open the dragons' mouths.

Growing

Snapdragons prefer **full sun** but tolerate light or partial shade. The soil should be **fertile, rich in organic matter** and **well drained**. These plants prefer a **neutral or alkaline** soil and will not perform as well in acidic soil. Do not cover seeds when sowing; they require light for germination.

To encourage bushy growth, pinch the tips of the young plants. Cut off the flower spikes as they fade to promote further blooming and to prevent the plant from dying back before the end of the season.

Tips

The height of the variety dictates the best place for it in a border—the shortest varieties work well near the front, and the tallest look good in the center or back. The dwarf and medium-height varieties can also be used in planters. A trailing variety does well in hanging baskets.

Recommended

There are many cultivars of **A. majus** available, generally grouped into three size categories: dwarf, medium and giant.

A. majus cultivars (above & below)

Snapdragons are perennial plants that are treated like annuals. Although they won't usually survive the winter here, they will often flower well into fall and may self-seed.

Features: white, cream, yellow, orange, red, maroon, pink, purple, some bicolored flowers
Height: 6"–4' **Spread:** 6–24"

Sweet Alyssum
Lobularia

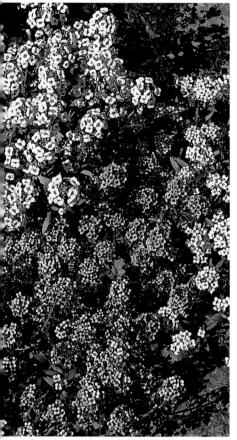

L. maritima cultivars (above & below)

Leave alyssum plants out all winter. In spring, remove the previous year's growth to expose self-sown seedlings below.

Sweet alyssum is excellent for creating soft edges, and it self-seeds, popping up along pathways and between stones late in the season to give summer a sweet send-off.

Growing

Sweet alyssum prefers **full sun** but tolerates light shade. **Well-drained** soil of **average fertility** is preferred, but poor soil is tolerated. Sweet alyssum may die back a bit during the heat and humidity of summer. Trim it back and water it periodically to encourage new growth and more flowers for when the weather cools.

Tips

Sweet alyssum creeps around rock gardens, over rock walls and along the edges of beds. It is an excellent choice for seeding into cracks and crevices of walkways and between patio stones, and once established it readily reseeds. It is also good for filling in spaces between taller plants in borders and mixed containers.

Recommended

L. maritima forms a low, spreading mound of foliage. The entire plant appears to be covered in tiny blossoms when in full flower. Cultivars with flowers in a wide range of colors are available.

Features: fragrant, pink, purple, yellow, salmon, white flowers **Height:** 3–12"
Spread: 6–24"

Sweet Potato Vine

Ipomoea

I. batatas 'Tricolor' (above), *I. batatas* 'Margarita' (below)

This vigorous rambling plant with lime green, bruised purple or green, pink and cream variegated leaves can make any gardener look like a genius.

Growing

Grow sweet potato vine in **full sun**. Any type of soil will do, but a **light, well-drained** soil of **poor fertility** is preferred.

Tips

Sweet potato vine is a great addition to mixed planters, window boxes and hanging baskets. In a rock garden it will scramble about, and along the top of a retaining wall it will cascade over the edge. Although this plant is a vine, its bushy habit and colorful leaves make it a useful foliage plant.

Recommended

I. batatas (sweet potato vine) is a twining climber that is grown for its attractive foliage rather than its flowers. Several cultivars are available.

As a bonus, when you pull up your plant at the end of summer, you can eat any tubers (sweet potatoes) that have formed.

Features: decorative foliage; insignificant flowers **Height:** about 12" **Spread:** up to 10'

Verbena

Verbena

V. bonariensis (above), *V. x hybrida* (below)

Verbenas offer butterflies a banquet. Butterfly visitors include tiger swallowtails, silver-spotted skippers, great spangled fritillaries and painted ladies.

Growing

Verbenas grow best in **full sun**. The soil should be **fertile** and very **well drained**. Pinch back young plants for bushy growth.

If plants become leggy or overgrown, cut them back by one-half to tidy them up and promote the production of lots of fall blooms.

Tips

Use verbenas on rock walls and in beds, borders, rock gardens, containers, hanging baskets and window boxes. They make good substitutes for ivy-leaved geranium, where the sun is hot and where a roof overhang keeps the mildew-prone verbenas dry.

Recommended

V. bonariensis forms a low clump of foliage from which tall, stiff stems bear clusters of small, purple flowers.

V. x hybrida is a bushy plant that may be upright or spreading. It bears clusters of small flowers in a wide range of colors. Cultivars are available.

Also called: garden verbena **Features:** red, pink, purple, blue, yellow, scarlet, silver, peach, white flowers; some with white centers
Height: 8"–5' **Spread:** 12–36"

Ajuga
Ajuga

Often labeled as rampant runners, ajugas grow best where they can roam freely. Although some species and cultivars are considered invasive in some states, well-behaved cultivars available.

Growing

Ajugas develop the best leaf color in **partial or light shade** but tolerate full shade. The leaves may become scorched when exposed to too much sun. Any **well-drained** soil is suitable. Divide these vigorous plants any time during the growing season. Remove any new growth or seedlings that don't show the hybrid leaf coloring.

Tips

Ajugas make excellent ground-covers for difficult sites, such as exposed slopes and dense shade. They are also attractive in shrub borders, where their dense growth will prevent the spread of all but the most tenacious weeds.

Recommended

A. genevensis (Geneva bugleweed) is an upright, noninvasive species that bears blue, white or pink spring flowers.

A. pyramidalis '**Metallica Crispa**' (upright bugleweed) is a very slow-growing plant with bronzy, crinkly foliage and violet-blue flowers.

A. reptans 'Caitlin's Giant' (above)
A. reptans 'Burgundy Glow' (below)

A. reptans is a low, quick-spreading groundcover. The many cultivars are grown for their colorful, often variegated foliage.

A x tenorii is a hybrid with a finer leaf texture, a very short habit and deep blue flowers. Look for the cultivars '**Chocolate Chip**' and '**Vanilla Chip.**'

Also called: bugleweed **Features:** purple, blue, pink, white, late-spring to early-summer flowers; colorful foliage **Height:** 3–12" **Spread:** 6–36" **Hardiness:** zones 3–8

Artemisia
Artemisia

A. schmidtiana 'Nana' (above)
A. ludoviciana 'Valerie Finnis' (below)

Most of the artemisias are valued for their silvery foliage, not their flowers. Silver is the ultimate blending color because it enhances every other hue combined with it.

Growing
Artemisias grow best in **full sun**. The soil should be of **low to**

average fertility and **well drained**. These plants dislike wet, humid conditions.

When artemisias begin to look straggly, cut them back hard to encourage new growth and maintain a neater form. Divide them every year or two, when plant clumps appear to be thinning in the centers.

Tips
Use artemisias in rock gardens and borders. Their silvery gray foliage makes them good backdrop plants to use behind brightly colored flowers. They are also useful for filling in spaces between other plants. Smaller forms may be used to create knot gardens. Artemisias can spread and become invasive in the garden.

Recommended
A. ludoviciana (white sage, silver sage) is an upright, clump-forming plant with silvery white foliage. The species is not grown as often as its cultivars. (Zones 4–8)

A. x 'Powis Castle' is a compact, mounding, shrubby plant with feathery, silvery gray foliage. This hybrid is reliably hardy to zone 6, but it can also grow in colder regions if planted with winter protection in a sheltered site.

A. schmidtiana (silvermound artemisia) is a low, dense, mound-forming perennial with feathery, hairy, silvery gray foliage. 'Nana' (dwarf silvermound) is very compact and grows only half the size of the species. (Zones 4–8)

Also called: wormwood, sage
Features: silvery gray, feathery or deeply lobed foliage **Height:** 6"–6' **Spread:** 12–36"
Hardiness: zones 3–8

Aster

Aster

Among the final plants to bloom before the snow flies, asters often provide a last meal for migrating butterflies. The purples and pinks of asters contrast with the yellow-flowered perennials common in the late-summer garden.

Growing

Asters prefer **full sun** but tolerate partial shade. The soil should be **fertile**, **moist** and **well drained**. Pinch or shear these plants back in early summer to promote dense growth and reduce disease problems. Mulch in winter to protect plants from temperature fluctuations. Divide every two or three years to maintain vigor and control spread.

Tips

Use asters in the middle of borders and in cottage gardens, or naturalize them in wild gardens.

Recommended

Some aster species have recently been reclassified under the genus *Symphyotrichum*. You may see both names at garden centers.

A. novae-angliae (Michaelmas daisy, New England aster) is an upright, spreading, clump-forming perennial that bears yellow-centered, purple flowers. Many cultivars are available.

A. novi-belgii (Michaelmas daisy, New York aster) is a dense, upright, clump-forming perennial with purple flowers. Many cultivars are available.

Features: late-summer to mid-autumn flowers in shades of red, white, blue, purple, pink; often with yellow centers **Height:** 10"–5' **Spread:** 18–36" **Hardiness:** zones 3–8

A. novi-belgii (above), *A. novae-angliae* (below)

What looks like a single flower of an aster, or other plants with daisy-like flowers, is actually a cluster of many tiny flowers. Look closely at the center of the flowerhead and you will see all the individual florets.

Astilbe

Astilbe

A. x *arendsii* cultivars (above), *A.* x *arendsii* 'Bressingham Beauty' (below)

Astilbes are beacons in the shade. Their high-impact flowers will brighten any gloomy section of your garden.

Growing

Astilbes grow best in **light or partial shade** but tolerate full shade, though they will not flower as much in full shade. The soil should be **fertile, humus rich, acidic, moist** and **well drained**. Although they appreciate moist soil, astilbes don't like standing water.

In late summer, transplant seedlings found near the parent plant to create plumes of color all through the garden.

Astilbes should be divided every three years or so to maintain plant vigor. Root masses may lift out of the soil as they mature. Add a layer of topsoil and mulch if this occurs.

Tips

Astilbes can be grown near the edges of bog gardens and ponds, and in woodland gardens and shaded borders.

Recommended

A. x *arendsii* (astilbe, false spirea, Arend's astilbe) is a group of hybrids with many available cultivars.

A. chinensis (Chinese astilbe) is a dense, vigorous perennial that tolerates dry soil better than other astilbe species. Many cultivars are available.

A. japonica (Japanese astilbe) is a compact, clump-forming perennial. The species is rarely grown in favor of the many cultivars.

Features: attractive foliage; white, pink, purple, peach, red summer flowers
Height: 10"–4' **Spread:** 8–36"
Hardiness: zones 3–9

Bearberry
Arctostaphylos

A. *uva-ursi* (above & below)

Bearberry forms an attractive, low-growing mat of evergreen foliage. The tiny flowers and bright red fruit provide a lovely contrast to the dark green leaves.

Growing

Bearberry grows well in **full sun** or **partial shade**. The soil should be of **poor to average fertility, well drained, acidic** and **moist**, though bearberry will adapt to alkaline soils.

Tips

Once established, bearberry is a vigorous, wide-spreading groundcover. It makes a good addition to rock gardens and mixed beds and borders. It can be grown on slopes that are difficult to mow as an alternative to grass. Mulch will keep the weeds down until bearberry establishes and fills in.

Recommended

A. ***uva-ursi*** is a low-growing, spreading, evergreen plant. It bears white to pink flowers in late spring followed by berries that ripen to bright red. Cultivars are available.

This plant's alternative common name, kinnikinnick, *is said to be an Algonquian term, meaning 'smoking mixture,' reflecting a traditional use for the leaves.*

Also called: kinnikinnick
Features: evergreen foliage; white to pink flowers; fruit; habit **Height:** 4–6"
Spread: 18–36" **Hardiness:** zones 2–7

Bellflower

Campanula

C. persicifolia (above), *C. carpatica* 'White Clips' (below)

Thanks to their wide range of heights and habits, it is possible to put bellflowers almost anywhere in the garden.

Growing

Bellflowers grow well in **full sun, partial shade** or **light shade**. The soil should be of **average to high fertility** and **well drained**. These plants appreciate a mulch to keep their roots cool and moist in summer and protected in winter, particularly if snow cover is inconsistent. Deadhead to prolong blooming.

Tips

Plant upright and mounding bellflowers in borders and cottage gardens. Use low, spreading and trailing bellflowers in rock gardens and on rock walls. You can also edge beds with the low-growing varieties.

Recommended

C. x **'Birch Hybrid'** is a low-growing and spreading plant. It bears light blue to mauve flowers in summer.

C. carpatica (Carpathian bellflower, Carpathian harebell) is a spreading, mounding perennial that bears blue, white or purple flowers in summer. Several cultivars are available.

C. glomerata (clustered bellflower) forms a clump of upright stems and bears clusters of purple, blue or white flowers throughout most of summer.

C. persicifolia (peach-leaved bellflower) is an upright perennial that bears white, blue or purple flowers from early summer to mid-summer.

C. poscharskyana (Serbian bellflower) is a trailing perennial that likes to wind its way around other plants. It bears light violet-blue flowers in summer and early autumn.

Also called: campanula **Features:** blue, white, purple, pink, spring, summer or autumn flowers; varied growing habits **Height:** 4"–6' **Spread:** 12–36" **Hardiness:** zones 3–7

Black-Eyed Susan

Rudbeckia

Black-eyed Susan is a tough, low-maintenance, long-lived perennial. Plant them in drifts to give your garden a casual appearance.

Growing

Black-eyed Susan grows well in **full sun** or **partial shade**. The soil should be of **average fertility** and **well drained**. Some *Rudbeckia* species are touted as 'claybusters' for their tolerance of fairly heavy clay soils. Established plants are drought tolerant but prefer to have a regular source of water. Divide them in fall every three to five years.

Tips

Include these native plants in wildflower and natural gardens, beds and borders. Pinching the plants in early June will encourage lower, bushier growth but can somewhat delay flowering.

Recommended

R. fulgida is an upright, spreading plant that bears orange-yellow flowers with brown centers. **Var. *sullivantii* 'Goldsturm'** bears large, golden yellow flowers.

R. laciniata (cutleaf coneflower) forms a large, open clump of stems and deeply cut leaves. The flowers are yellow with green centers. **'Goldquelle'** has bright yellow, double flowers.

R. nitida is an upright, spreading plant with green-centered, yellow flowers. **'Herbstsonne'** ('Autumn Sun') has golden yellow flowers.

R. fulgida with purple coneflower (above)
R. nitida 'Herbstsonne' (below)

Cultivars of R. hirta are often grown as annuals, offering plentiful blooms in a wider range of colors.

Features: yellow or orange-yellow flowers with brown or green centers; foliage; easy to grow
Height: 2–6' **Spread:** 18–36"
Hardiness: zones 3–8

Bleeding Heart

Dicentra

D. formosa (above), *D. spectabilis* (below)

All bleeding hearts contain toxic alkaloids, and some people develop allergic skin reactions from contact with these plants.

Every garden should have a bleeding heart plant. Tucked away in a shady spot, this lovely plant appears in spring and fills the garden with fresh promise.

Growing

Bleeding hearts prefer **light shade** but tolerate partial or full shade. The soil should be **humus rich, moist** and **well drained**. Very dry summer conditions cause the plants to die back, though they will revive in autumn or the following spring. Bleeding hearts must remain moist while blooming in order to prolong the flowering period.

Tips

Bleeding hearts can be naturalized in a woodland garden or grown in a border or rock garden. They make excellent early-season specimen plants and do well near ponds or streams.

Recommended

D. eximia (fringed bleeding heart) forms a loose, mounded clump of lacy, fern-like foliage and bears pink or white flowers in spring and sporadically over summer.

D. formosa (western bleeding heart) is a low-growing, wide-spreading plant with pink flowers that fade to white as they mature. The most drought tolerant of the bleeding hearts, it is the most likely to continue flowering all summer.

D. spectabilis (common bleeding heart, Japanese bleeding heart) forms a large, elegant mound that bears flowers with white inner petals and pink outer petals. Several cultivars are available.

Features: pink, white, red, purple spring and summer flowers; attractive foliage
Height: 1–4' **Spread:** 12–36"
Hardiness: zones 3–9

Bugbane

Cimicifuga

Bugbanes put on impressive displays. These tall plants bear fragrant flowers above decorative foliage.

Growing

Bugbanes grow best in **partial or light shade**. The soil should be **fertile, humus rich** and **moist**. The plants may require support from a peony hoop. The plants spread by rhizomes; small pieces of root can be carefully unearthed and replanted in spring if more plants are desired.

Tips

Bugbanes make attractive additions to an open woodland garden, shaded border or pondside planting. They don't compete well with tree roots or other plants that have vigorous roots. Bugbanes are worth growing close to the house because the late-season flowers are wonderfully fragrant.

Recommended

C. racemosa (black snakeroot) is a clump-forming perennial with long-stemmed spikes of fragrant, creamy white flowers.

C. simplex (Kamchatka bugbane) is a clump-forming perennial with fragrant bottlebrush-like spikes of flowers. Several cultivars are available, including those with bronze or purple foliage.

C. simplex 'Brunette' (above), *C. racemosa* (below)

C. racemosa is also known as black cohosh, and the rhizomes are used in herbal medicine.

Also called: snakeroot
Features: fragrant, white, cream, pink late-summer and autumn flowers, some with bronze or purple foliage **Height:** 3–8'
Spread: 24" **Hardiness:** zones 3–8

Chrysanthemum
Chrysanthemum

C. x *superbum* (above & below)

Although the name Chrysanthemum *comes from the Greek and means 'golden flower,' these plants actually bloom in a wide range of bright colors.*

This huge family of plants have daisy-like flowers in common, despite the many botanical name changes that plants in the genus have undergone in recent years.

Growing

Chrysanthemums grow best in **full sun**. The soil should be **fertile, moist** and **well drained**. Pinch plants back in early summer to encourage bushy growth and increase flower production. Divide plants every two or three years to keep them growing vigorously.

Tips

Chrysanthemums provide a blaze of color in the summer and fall garden. In groups or as specimen plants they can be included in borders and planters or in plantings close to the house. Plants purchased in fall can be added to spots where summer annuals have faded.

Recommended

C. x *rubellum* **'Clara Curtis'** is a bushy plant that bears semi-double pink flowers with yellow centers in mid- to late summer.

C. x *superbum* (*Leucanthemum* x *superbum*; shasta daisy) is a clump-forming plant that bears abundant, white, daisy-like flowers with yellow centers in summer and early fall. There are many cultivars available with single or double flowers and some have decorative, frilled or twisted petals.

Features: summer or fall flowers in shades of white, orange, red, yellow, pink, red, purple; habit **Height:** 30–36" **Spread:** 24" **Hardiness:** zones 5–9

Columbine

Aquilegia

Delicate and beautiful columbines add a touch of simple elegance to any garden. Blooming from the cool of spring through to mid-summer, these long-lasting flowers herald the passing of spring and the arrival of warm summer weather.

Growing

Columbines grow well in **light or partial shade**. They prefer soil that is **fertile, moist** and **well drained**, but they adapt to most soil conditions. Division is not required but can be done to propagate desirable plants. The divided plants may take a while to recover, because columbines dislike having their roots disturbed.

Tips

Use columbines in rock gardens, formal or casual borders and naturalized or woodland gardens.

Recommended

A. canadensis (wild columbine, Canada columbine) is a native plant that is common in woodlands and fields. It bears yellow flowers with red spurs.

A. x *hybrida* (*A.* x *cultorum*; hybrid columbine) forms mounds of delicate foliage and has exceptional flowers. Many hybrids have been developed with showy flowers in a wide range of colors.

A. vulgaris (European columbine, common columbine) has been used to develop many hybrids and cultivars with flowers in a variety of colors.

Features: red, yellow, pink, purple, blue, white spring and summer flowers; color of spurs often differs from that of the petals; attractive foliage **Height:** 18–36" **Spread:** 12–24" **Hardiness:** zones 3–9

A. canadensis (above)
A. x *hybrida* 'McKana Giants' (below)

Columbines self-seed but are not invasive. Each year, a few new seedlings may turn up near the parent plant and can be transplanted.

Coreopsis

Coreopsis

C. verticillata 'Moonbeam' (above), *C. auriculata* (below)

These plants produce flowers all summer and are easy to grow; they make a fabulous addition to every garden.

Growing

Coreopsis grows best in **full sun**. The soil should be of **average fertility, sandy, light** and **well drained**. Plants can develop crown rot in moist, cool locations with heavy soil. Too fertile a soil will encourage floppy growth. Deadhead to keep plants blooming.

Tips

Coreopsis are versatile plants, useful in formal and informal borders and in meadow plantings and cottage gardens. They look best when planted in groups.

Recommended

C. auriculata **'Nana'** (mouse-eared tickseed) is a low-growing species, well suited to rock gardens and the fronts of borders. It grows about 12" tall and spreads indefinitely, though slowly. It bears yellow-orange flowers in late spring.

C. verticillata (thread-leaf coreopsis) is a mound-forming plant with attractive, finely divided foliage and bright yellow flowers. It grows 24–32" tall and spreads 18". Available cultivars include **'Moonbeam,'** which forms a mound of delicate, lacy foliage and bears creamy yellow flowers.

Also called: tickseed **Features:** yellow, yellow-orange summer flowers; attractive foliage **Height:** 12–32" **Spread:** 12–24" **Hardiness:** zones 3–9

Daylily
Hemerocallis

The daylily's adaptability and durability combined with its variety in color, blooming period, size and texture explain this perennial's popularity.

Growing

Daylilies grow in any light from **full sun to full shade**. The deeper the shade, the fewer flowers will be produced. The soil should be **fertile, moist** and **well drained**, but these plants adapt to most conditions and are hard to kill once established. They can be left indefinitely without dividing, or can be divided every two or three years to keep plants vigorous and to propagate them. Deadhead to prolong the blooming period.

Tips

Plant daylilies alone, or group them in borders, on banks and in ditches to control erosion. They can be naturalized in woodland or meadow gardens. Small varieties are nice in planters.

Recommended

Daylilies come in an almost infinite number of forms, sizes and colors in a range of species, cultivars and hybrids. See your local garden center or daylily grower to find out what's available. Ask for field-grown daylilies as they adapt quickly.

H. 'Dewey Roquemore' (above), *H.* 'Bonanza' (below)

Be careful when deadheading purple-flowered daylilies because the sap can stain fingers and clothes.

Features: spring and summer flowers in every color except blue and pure white; grass-like foliage **Height:** 1–4' **Spread:** 1–4' **Hardiness:** zones 2–9

False Indigo

Baptisia

B. australis (above & below)

*A*ttractive green foliage and spikes of bright blue flowers in early summer make this plant a worthy addition, even if it does take up a sizable amount of garden real estate.

If you've had difficulties growing lupines, try the far less demanding false indigo instead.

Growing

False indigo prefers **full sun** but tolerates partial shade. Too much shade causes lank growth that flops over easily. The soil should be of **poor to average fertility, sandy** and **well drained**. False indigo doesn't need dividing and resents transplanting as it doesn't like having its roots disturbed.

Tips

False indigo can be used in an informal border or cottage garden. It is an attractive addition for a naturalized planting, on a slope, or in any sunny, well-drained spot in the garden.

Recommended

B. australis is an upright or somewhat spreading, clump-forming plant that bears spikes of purple-blue flowers in early summer.

Features: purple-blue late-spring or early-summer flowers; habit; foliage **Height:** 3–5' **Spread:** 2–4' **Hardiness:** zones 3–9

Fescue

Festuca

F. glauca 'Elijah Blue' (above), *F. glauca* (below)

This fine-leaved ornamental grass forms tufted clumps that resemble pin cushions. Its metallic blue coloring adds an all-season cooling accent to the garden.

Growing

Fescue thrives in **full sun to light shade**. The soil should be of **average fertility**, **moist** and **well drained**. Plants are drought tolerant once established. Fescue emerges early in the spring, so shear it back to 1" above the crown in late winter, before new growth emerges. Shear off flower stalks just above the foliage to keep the plants tidy and to prevent self-seeding.

Tips

With its fine texture and distinct blue color, this grass can be used as a single specimen in a rock garden or a container planting. Plant fescue in drifts to create a sea of blue or a handsome edge to a bed, border or pathway. It looks attractive in both formal and informal gardens.

Recommended

F. glauca forms tidy, tufted clumps of fine, blue-toned foliage and panicles of flowers in May and June. Cultivars and hybrids come in varying heights and in shades ranging from blue to olive green. **'Elijah Blue,' 'Boulder Blue,' 'Skinner's Blue'** and **'Solling'** are popular selections.

Also called: blue fescue **Features:** blue to blue-green foliage; color that persists into winter; habit **Height:** 6–12" **Spread:** 10–12" **Hardiness:** zones 3–9

Flowering Fern
Osmunda

O. regalis (above), *O. cinnamomea* (below)

The flowering fern's 'flowers' are actually its spore-producing sporangia.

Ferns have a prehistoric mystique and add a graceful elegance and textural accent to the garden.

Growing

Flowering ferns prefer **light shade** but tolerate full sun if the soil is consistently moist. The soil should be **fertile, humus rich, acidic** and **moist**. Flowering ferns tolerate wet soil, and they will spread as offsets form at the plant bases.

Tips

These large ferns form an attractive mass when planted in large colonies. They can be included in beds and borders and are a welcome addition to a woodland garden.

Recommended

O. cinnamomea (cinnamon fern) has light green fronds that fan out in a circular fashion from a central point. Bright green, leafless, fertile fronds that mature to cinnamon brown are produced in spring and stand straight up in the center of the plant. (Zones 2–8)

O. regalis (royal fern) forms a dense clump of foliage. Feathery, flower-like, rusty brown fertile fronds stand out among the sterile fronds. **'Purpurescens'** fronds are purple-red when they emerge in spring and mature to green. This contrasts well with the purple stems. (Zones 3–9)

Features: perennial deciduous fern; decorative, fertile fronds; habit **Height:** 30"–5'
Spread: 24–36" **Hardiness:** zones 2–9

Foamflower

Tiarella

T. cordifolia (above & below)

Foamflowers form handsome groundcovers in shaded areas, with their attractive leaves and delicate, starry, white flowers.

Growing

Foamflowers prefer **partial, light or full shade** without afternoon sun. The soil should be **humus rich, moist** and **slightly acidic**. These plants adapt to most soils. Divide in spring. Deadhead to encourage re-blooming. If the foliage fades or develops rust in summer, cut it partway to the ground. New growth will emerge.

Tips

Foamflowers are excellent groundcovers for shaded and woodland gardens. They can be included in shaded borders and left to naturalize in wild gardens.

Features: white or pink spring and sometimes early-summer flowers; decorative foliage
Height: 4–12" **Spread:** 12–24"
Hardiness: zones 3–8

Recommended

T. cordifolia is a low-growing, spreading plant that bears spikes of foamy-looking, white flowers. Cultivars are available.

T. **'Maple Leaf'** is a clump-forming hybrid with bronze-green, maple-like leaves and pink-flushed flowers.

These plants spread by underground stems, which can be easily pulled up to stop excessive spread.

Fountain Grass

Pennisetum

P. setaceum 'Rubrum'

ountain grass' low-maintenance needs and graceful form make it easy to place. It will soften any landscape, even in winter.

Growing

Fountain grass thrives in **full sun**. The soil should be of **average fertility** and **well drained**. Plants are drought tolerant once established. Plants may self-seed but are not troublesome. Shear back perennial selections in early spring, and divide them when they start to die out in the center.

Tips

Fountain grass can be used as individual specimen plants, in group plantings and drifts or combined with flowering annuals, perennials, shrubs and other ornamental grasses. Annual selections are often planted in containers or beds for height and stature.

Recommended

Both perennial and annual fountain grasses exist. Popular perennials include *P. alopecuroides* '**Hameln**' (dwarf perennial fountain grass), a compact cultivar with silvery white plumes and narrow, dark green foliage that turns gold in fall, and *P. orientale* (Oriental fountain grass), with tall, blue-green foliage and large, silvery white flowers. (Zones 6–9, with winter protection)

Annual fountain grasses include *P. glaucum* '**Purple Majesty**' (purple ornamental millet), which has blackish purple foliage and coarse, bottlebrush flowers. Its form resembles a corn stalk. *P. setaceum* (annual fountain grass) has narrow green foliage and pinkish purple flowers that mature to gray. Its cultivar '**Rubrum**' (red annual fountain grass) has broader, deep burgundy foliage and pinkish purple flowers.

Features: arching, fountain-like habit; silvery pink, dusty rose to purplish black foliage; white or pinkish purple flowers; winter interest **Height:** 2–5' **Spread:** 24–36" **Hardiness:** zones 5–9 (some species are annuals)

Goat's Beard

Aruncus

Despite its imposing size, goat's beard has a soft and delicate appearance, with its divided foliage and large, plume-like, cream-colored flowers.

Growing

This plant prefers **partial to full shade**. If planted in deep shade, it will bear fewer blooms. It tolerates some full sun as long as the soil is kept evenly moist and it is protected from the afternoon sun. The soil should be **fertile, moist** and **humus rich**.

Tips

Goat's beard looks very natural growing near the sunny entrance or edge of a woodland garden, in a native plant garden or in a large island planting. It may also be used in a border or alongside a stream or pond.

Recommended

A. aethusifolius (dwarf Korean goat's beard) forms a low-growing, compact mound and bears branched spikes of loosely held, cream flowers.

A. dioicus (giant goat's beard, common goat's beard) is a large, bushy, shrub-like perennial with large plumes of creamy white flowers. There are several cultivars.

A. dioicus (above & below)

Male and female flowers are produced on separate plants. In general, male flowers are full and fuzzy, whereas female flowers are more pendulous, but it can be difficult to tell the two apart.

Features: cream or white early to mid-summer blooms; shrub-like habit; attractive foliage and seedheads **Height:** 6"–6' **Spread:** 1–6' **Hardiness:** zones 3–7

Hardy Geranium
Geranium

G. sanguineum (above), *G. sanguineum* var. *striatum* (below)

There is a type of geranium that suits every garden, thanks to the beauty and diversity of this hardy plant.

Growing
Hardy geraniums grow well in **full sun, partial shade** or **light shade**. These plants dislike hot weather and prefer soil of **average fertility** with **good drainage**. *G. renardii* prefers a poor, well-drained soil. Divide plants in spring.

Tips
These long-flowering plants are great in a border. They fill in the spaces between shrubs and other larger plants and keep the weeds down. They can be included in rock gardens and woodland gardens, or mass planted as groundcovers.

Recommended
G. 'Brookside' is a clump-forming, drought-tolerant geranium with finely cut leaves and deep blue to violet-blue flowers.

G. macrorrhizum (bigroot geranium, scented cranesbill) forms a spreading mound of fragrant foliage and bears flowers in various shades of pink. Cultivars are available.

G. renardii (Renard's geranium) forms a clump of velvety, deeply veined, crinkled foliage. A few purple-veined white flowers appear over summer, but the foliage remains the main attraction.

G. sanguineum (bloodred cranesbill, bloody cranesbill) forms a dense, mounding clump and bears bright magenta flowers. Many cultivars are available.

Also called: cranesbill geranium
Features: white, red, pink, purple, blue summer flowers; attractive, sometimes-fragrant foliage **Height:** 4–36" **Spread:** 12–36"
Hardiness: zones 3–8

Heuchera
Heuchera

From soft yellow-greens and oranges to midnight purples and silvery, dappled maroons, heucheras offer a great variety of foliage options for a perennial garden with partial shade.

Growing

Heucheras grow best in **light or partial shade**. The foliage colors can bleach out in full sun, and plants grow leggy in full shade. The soil should be of **average to rich fertility, humus rich, neutral to alkaline, moist** and **well drained**. Good air circulation is essential. Deadhead to prolong the bloom.

Heucheras should be dug up every two or three years and the oldest, woodiest roots and stems removed. Plants may be divided at this time, if desired, then replanted with the crown at or just above soil level.

Tips

Grown for their foliage more than their flowers, heucheras are useful individually or in groups as edging plants, in woodland gardens or as groundcovers in low-traffic areas. Combine different foliage types for an interesting display.

Recommended

There are dozens of beautiful cultivars available with almost limitless variations of foliage markings and colors. See your local garden center or view a mail-order catalog to see what's available.

H. x brizioides 'Firefly' (above), *H. sanguineum* (below)

Heucheras have a strange habit of pushing themselves up out of the soil because of their shallow root systems. Mulch in autumn if the plants begin heaving from the ground.

Also called: coral bells, alumroot
Features: very decorative foliage; red, pink, white, yellow, purple spring or summer flowers
Height: 1–4' **Spread:** 6–18"
Hardiness: zones 3–9

Hosta
Hosta

H. fortunei 'Francee'

Some gardeners think the flowers clash with the foliage, and they remove the flower stems when they first emerge. If you find the flowers unattractive, removing them won't harm the plant.

Hostas are the number one perennial in the United States. Breeders are always looking for new variations in hosta foliage. Swirls, stripes, puckers and ribs enhance the leaves' various sizes, shapes and colors.

Growing

Hostas prefer **light or partial shade** but will grow in full shade. Morning sun is preferable to afternoon sun in partial shade situations. The soil should ideally be **fertile, moist** and **well drained**, but most soils are tolerated. Hostas are fairly drought tolerant, especially if given a mulch to help retain moisture.

Division is not required but can be done every few years in spring or summer to propagate new plants.

Tips

Hostas make wonderful woodland plants and look very attractive when combined with ferns and other fine-textured plants. Hostas are also good plants for a mixed border, particularly when used to hide the ugly, leggy, lower stems and branches of some shrubs. Hostas' dense growth and thick, shade-providing leaves allow them to suppress weeds.

Recommended

Hostas have been subjected to a great deal of crossbreeding and hybridizing, resulting in hundreds of cultivars. Two popular cultivars are *H.* **'Elegans'** and *H. fortunei* **'Francee.'** Visit your local garden center or get a mail-order catalog to find out what's available.

Features: decorative foliage; white or purple summer and autumn flowers **Height:** 4–36" **Spread:** 6"–6' **Hardiness:** zones 3–8

Iris

Iris

Irises are steeped in history and lore. Irises come in all the colors of the rainbow, and the name iris is from the Greek, meaning rainbow.

Growing
Irises prefer **full sun** but tolerate very light or dappled shade. The soil should be of **average fertility** and **well drained**. Japanese iris and Siberian iris prefer a moist but still well-drained soil. Divide in late summer or early autumn. Deadhead irises to keep them tidy. Cut back the foliage of Siberian iris in spring.

Tips
All irises are popular border plants, but Japanese iris and Siberian iris are also useful alongside streams or ponds. Dwarf cultivars make attractive additions to rock gardens.

Recommended
There are many iris species and hybrids available. Among the most popular is the bearded iris, often a hybrid of **I. germanica**. It has the widest range of flower colors but is susceptible to attack from the iris borer, which can kill a plant. Several irises are not susceptible, including Japanese iris (*I. ensata*) and Siberian iris (*I. sibirica*). Check with your local garden center to find out what is available.

I. sibirica (above), *I. germanica* 'Stepping Out' (below)

Wash your hands after handling irises because they can cause severe internal irritation if ingested.

Features: spring, summer and sometimes autumn flowers in many shades of pink, red, purple, blue, white, brown, yellow; attractive foliage **Height:** 4"–4' **Spread:** 6"–4' **Hardiness:** zones 3–10

Lungwort
Pulmonaria

P. saccharata (above & below)

The wide array of lungworts have highly attractive foliage that range in color from apple green to silver-spotted and olive to dark emerald.

Growing

Lungworts prefer **partial to full shade**. The soil should be **fertile, humus rich, moist** and **well drained**. Rot can occur in very wet soil.

Divide in early summer after flowering or in autumn. Provide the newly planted divisions with a lot of water to help them re-establish.

To keep lungworts tidy and show off the fabulous foliage, deadhead the plants by shearing them back lightly after they flower.

Tips

Lungworts make attractive groundcovers for shady borders, woodland gardens and pond and stream edges.

Recommended

P. longifolia (long-leaved lungwort) forms a dense clump of long, narrow, white-spotted green leaves and bears clusters of blue flowers.

P. officinalis (common lungwort, spotted dog) forms a loose clump of evergreen foliage, spotted with white. The flowers open pink and mature to blue. Cultivars are available.

P. saccharata (Bethlehem sage) forms a compact clump of large, white-spotted, evergreen leaves and purple, red or white flowers. Many cultivars are available.

Features: decorative, mottled foliage; blue, red, pink, white spring flowers **Height:** 8–24" **Spread:** 8–36" **Hardiness:** zones 3–8

Maidenhair Fern

Adiantum

A. pedatum (above & below)

These charming and delicate-looking native ferns add a graceful touch to any woodland planting. Their unique habit and texture really make them stand out.

Growing

Maidenhair fern grows well in **light or partial shade** but tolerates full shade. The soil should be of **average fertility, humus rich, slightly acidic** and **moist**. This plant rarely needs dividing, but it can be divided in spring to propagate more plants.

Tips

These lovely ferns will do well in any shaded spot in the garden. Include them in rock or woodland gardens, in shaded borders and beneath shade trees. They are also an attractive addition to a shaded planting next to a water feature or on a slope where the foliage can be seen when it sways in the breeze.

Recommended

*A. **pedatum*** forms a spreading mound of delicate, arching fronds. Light green leaflets stand out against the black stems, and the whole plant turns bright yellow in fall. Spores are produced on the undersides of the leaflets.

Try growing the fine-textured and delicate maidenhair fern with varieties of hosta, pulmonaria *(lungwort) and* brunnera, *and enjoy the lovely contrast in texture.*

Also called: northern maidenhair
Features: deciduous perennial fern; summer and fall foliage; habit **Height:** 12–24"
Spread: 12–24" **Hardiness:** zones 2–8

Marsh Marigold

Caltha

C. palustris (above & below)

Marsh marigolds are harbingers of spring, offering glossy green leaves and bright yellow flowers when most other plants have barely started to sprout.

Growing

Marsh marigolds grow well in **full sun** or **partial shade**. The soil should be of **average fertility** and **moist**. These plants tolerate wet or periodically flooded soil

Marsh marigolds go dormant in mid-summer, and unfortunately many have been dug up and thrown out by gardeners who assume that they are dead.

and are often found growing next to or in streams, ponds and lakes. Plants often die back and go dormant in summer. Divide every two or three years after flowering has finished in spring.

Tips

Marsh marigold is a beautiful native plant that makes an excellent addition to areas of the garden that stay damp or wet. When grown in borders, they should be kept well watered. Plant them with plants that are slow to start in spring but that will fill in the space left when marsh marigold becomes dormant in mid-summer.

Recommended

C. palustris forms a low mound of glossy, heart-shaped leaves. Yellow flowers are produced in spring. Cultivars with double flowers or white flowers are also available.

Features: yellow or white spring flowers; attractive foliage **Height:** 8–16"
Spread: 10–20" **Hardiness:** zones 2–8

Meadow Rue

Thalictrum

Meadow rues are tall without being overbearing. Their fluffy flowers sway gracefully in the wind on wiry stems above fine foliage.

Growing

Meadow rues prefer **light or partial shade** but tolerate full sun with moist soil. The soil should be **humus rich, moist** and **well drained**. Meadow rues don't like being disturbed and may take a while to re-establish once they have been divided.

Tips

Meadow rues look beautiful when naturalized in an open woodland or meadow garden. In the middle or at the back of a border, they make a soft backdrop for bolder plants and flowers.

These plants often do not emerge until quite late in spring. Mark where you plant them so that you do not inadvertently disturb the roots while cultivating their bed before they begin to grow.

Recommended

T. aquilegifolium (columbine meadow rue) forms an upright mound with pink or white plumes of flowers. Cultivars are available.

T. rochebruneanum **'Lavender Mist'** (lavender mist meadow rue) forms a narrow, upright clump. The blooms are lavender purple and have numerous, distinctive yellow stamens.

T. rochebruneanum 'Lavender Mist' (above)
T. aquilegifolium (below)

Taller meadow rues may need some support if they are in an exposed location where a good wind can topple them.

Features: pink, purple, yellow, white summer flowers; light, airy habit; attractive foliage
Height: 2–5' **Spread:** 12–36"
Hardiness: zones 3–8

Meadowsweet

Filipendula

F. rubra (above), F. ulmaria (below)

Deadhead meadowsweets if you so desire,
but the faded seedheads are quite
attractive when left in place.

For an impressive, informal, vertical accent and showy clusters of fluffy, fragrant flowers, meadowsweet plants are second to none.

Growing

Meadowsweets prefer **partial or light shade** but tolerate full sun if the soil remains sufficiently moist. **Fertile, deep, humus rich** and **moist** soil is best, except in the case of *F. vulgaris*, which prefers dry soil. Divide in spring or autumn.

Tips

Most meadowsweets are excellent plants for bog gardens or wet sites. Grow them alongside streams or in moist meadows. Meadowsweets may also be grown in the back of a border, as long as they are kept well watered. Grow *F. vulgaris* if you can't provide the moisture needed by the other species.

Recommended

F. rubra (queen-of-the-prairie) forms a large, spreading clump and bears clusters of fragrant, pink flowers. Cultivars are available.

F. ulmaria (queen-of-the-meadow) forms a mounding clump and bears creamy white flowers in large clusters. Cultivars are available.

F. vulgaris (dropwort, meadowsweet) is a low-growing species that bears clusters of fragrant, creamy white flowers. Cultivars with double or pink flowers or variegated foliage are available.

Features: white, cream, pink, red late-spring or summer flowers; attractive foliage
Height: 2–8' **Spread:** 18"–4'
Hardiness: zones 3–8

Miscanthus
Miscanthus

Miscanthus is one of the most popular and majestic of all the ornamental grasses. Its graceful foliage dances in the wind and makes an impressive sight all year long.

Growing

Miscanthus prefers **full sun**. The soil should be of **average fertility**, **moist** and **well drained**, though some selections tolerate wet soil. All selections are drought tolerant once established. Leave the foliage in place to provide winter interest and then cut it back in spring before the new growth starts.

Tips

Give these magnificent beauties room to spread so you can fully appreciate their form. The plant's height will determine the best place for each selection in the border. They create dramatic impact in groups or as seasonal screens.

Recommended

There are many cultivars of **M. *sinensis***, all distinguished by the white midrib on the leaf blade. Some popular selections include **'Gracillimus'** (maiden grass), with long, fine-textured leaves; **'Grosse Fontaine'** (large fountain), a tall, wide-spreading, early-flowering selection; **'Morning Light'** (variegated maiden grass), a short, delicate plant with fine, white leaf edges; **var. *purpurescens*** (flame grass), with foliage that turns bright orange in early fall; **'Strictus'**

M. sinensis var. *purpurescens* (above)
M. sinensis cultivar (below)

(porcupine grass), a tall, stiff, upright selection with unusual horizontal yellow bands; and **'Zebrinus'** (zebra grass), an arching grass with horizontal yellow bands on the leaves.

Also called: eulalia, Japanese silver grass
Features: upright, arching habit; colorful summer and fall foliage; pink, copper, silver late-summer and fall flowers; winter interest
Height: 4–8' **Spread:** 2–4'
Hardiness: zones 5–8; zone 4 with protection

Ostrich Fern

Matteuccia

M. struthiopteris (above & below)

These popular, classic ferns are revered for their delicious, emerging spring fronds and their stately, vase-shaped habit.

Growing

Ostrich fern prefers **partial or light shade** but tolerates full shade or even full sun if the soil is kept moist. The soil should be **average to fertile**, **humus rich**, **neutral to acidic** and **moist**. Leaves may scorch if the soil is not moist enough. These ferns are aggressive spreaders that reproduce by spores. Unwanted plants can be pulled up and composted or given away.

Tips

This fern appreciates a moist woodland garden and is often found growing wild alongside woodland streams and creeks. Useful in shaded borders, these plants are quick to spread, to the delight of those who enjoy the young fronds as a culinary delicacy.

Recommended

M. struthiopteris (*M. pennsylvanica*) forms a circular cluster of slightly arching, feathery fronds. Stiff, brown, fertile fronds that are covered in reproductive spores stick up in the center of the cluster in late summer and persist through winter. They are popular for dried-flower arrangements.

Also called: fiddlehead fern
Features: perennial fern; foliage; habit
Height: 3–5' **Spread:** 12–36" or more
Hardiness: zones 1–8

Peony
Paeonia

From the simple, single flowers to the extravagant doubles, it's easy to become mesmerized with these voluptuous plants.

Growing

Peonies prefer **full sun** but tolerate some shade. The planting site should be well prepared before the plants are introduced. Peonies like **fertile, humus-rich, moist, well-drained** soil to which a lot of compost has been added. Mulch peonies lightly with compost in spring. Too much fertilizer, particularly nitrogen, causes floppy growth and retards blooming. Division is not required but can be done in autumn to propagate plants. Deadhead to keep plants looking tidy.

P. *lactiflora* 'Shimmering Velvet' (above), P. *lactiflora* cultivars (below)

Tips

These wonderful plants look great in a border combined with other early bloomers. They may be underplanted with bulbs and other plants that will die down by mid-summer—the emerging foliage of peonies hides the dying foliage of spring plants. Avoid planting peonies under trees, where they will have to compete for moisture and nutrients.

Tubers planted too shallow or, more commonly, too deep, will not flower. The buds or eyes on the tuber should be 1–2" below the soil surface.

Place wire cages around the plants in early spring to support the heavy flowers.

Recommended

There are hundreds of peonies available. Cultivars come in a wide range of colors, may have single or double flowers, and may or may not be fragrant. Visit your local garden center to see what is available.

Features: white, cream, yellow, pink, red, purple spring and early-summer flowers; attractive foliage **Height:** 24–32"
Spread: 24–32" **Hardiness:** zones 2–7

Phlox

Phlox

P. subulata (above), P. paniculata (below)

Phlox comes in many shapes and sizes, from low creepers to tall, bushy border plants. Its fragrant flowers come in a range of colors with blooming times from early spring to mid-autumn.

Growing

P. maculata and *P. paniculata* prefer **full sun,** *P. subulata* favors **full sun to partial**

shade, and *P. stolonifera* grows best in **partial shade to light shade.** All like **fertile, humus-rich, moist, well-drained** soil. Divide in autumn or spring.

Tips

Low-growing species look good in rock gardens, at the front of borders or cascading over retaining walls. Taller phloxes can be used in the middle of borders and are particularly effective when planted in groups.

Recommended

P. maculata (meadow phlox, wild sweet William) forms an upright clump of hairy stems with narrow leaves that are sometimes spotted with red. Pink, purple or white early-summer flowers are borne in conical clusters.

P. paniculata (garden phlox, summer phlox) is a tall, upright summer- and fall-blooming plant with many cultivars in various sizes and flower colors. Look for powdery mildew-resistant cultivars, like **'David,'** a beautiful white-flowered cultivar.

P. stolonifera (creeping phlox) is a low, spreading plant that bears flowers in several shades of purple in spring.

P. subulata (moss phlox, moss pink) is very low growing. Its flowers come in various colors and blanket the evergreen foliage. A light shearing after the plant finishes flowering in June will encourage tidy growth and possibly a second flush of flowers.

Features: white, blue, purple, orange, pink, red spring, summer or autumn flowers
Height: 2"–4' **Spread:** 12–36"
Hardiness: zones 3–8

Pinks
Dianthus

D. deltoides (above), D. plumarius (below)

From tiny and delicate to large and robust, this genus contains a wide variety of plants, many with spice-scented flowers.

Growing

Pinks prefer **full sun** but tolerate some light shade. A **well-drained, neutral or alkaline** soil is required. The most important factor in the successful cultivation of pinks is drainage—they hate to stand in water. Rocky outcroppings make up the native habitat of many species.

Tips

Pinks make excellent plants for rock gardens and rock walls, and for edging flower borders and walkways. They can also be used in cutting gardens and even as groundcovers. To prolong blooming, deadhead as the flowers fade, but leave a few flowers in place to go to seed.

Recommended

D. x *allwoodii* (allwood pinks) is a hybrid that forms a compact mound and bears flowers in a wide range of colors. Many cultivars are available.

D. deltoides (maiden pink) forms a mat of foliage and flowers in shades of red and pink.

D. gratianopolitanus (cheddar pink) is long-lived and forms a very dense mat of evergreen, silver gray foliage with sweet-scented flowers mostly in shades of pink.

D. plumarius (cottage pink) is note-worthy for its role in the development of many popular cultivars known collectively as garden pinks. The flowers can be single, semi-double or fully double and are available in many colors.

Features: sometimes-fragrant pink, red, white, purple spring or summer flowers; attractive foliage **Height:** 2–18" **Spread:** 6–24" **Hardiness:** zones 3–9

Purple Coneflower
Echinacea

E. purpurea (above & below)

Purple coneflower attracts wildlife to the garden, providing pollen, nectar and seeds to various hungry visitors.

Purple coneflower is a visual delight with its mauve petals offset by a spiky, orange center.

Growing

Purple coneflower grows well in **full sun** or very **light shade**. It tolerates any **well-drained** soil but prefers an **average to rich** soil. The thick tap-roots make this plant drought resist-ant, but it prefers to have regular water. Divide every four years or so in spring or fall.

Deadhead early in the flowering sea-son to prolong blooming. Later you may wish to leave the flowerheads in place to self-seed to provide winter interest. Pinch plants back or thin out the stems in early summer to encourage bushy growth that is less prone to mildew.

Tips

Use purple coneflowers in meadow gardens and informal borders, either in groups or as single specimens.

The dry flowerheads make an inter-esting feature in autumn and winter gardens.

Recommended

E. purpurea is an upright plant cov-ered in prickly hairs. It bears purple flowers with orangy centers. Culti-vars are available, including several popular new varieties with yellow or orange flowers.

Also called: coneflower, echinacea
Features: purple, pink, white, yellow, orange mid-summer to autumn flowers with rusty orange centers; persistent seedheads
Height: 2–5' **Spread:** 12–24"
Hardiness: zones 3–8

Reed Grass
Calamagrostis

C. x *acutiflora* 'Karl Foerster' (above & below)

This graceful, metamorphic grass changes its habit and flower color throughout the seasons. The slightest breeze keeps reed grass in perpetual motion.

Growing

Reed grass grows best in **full sun**. The soil should be **fertile, moist** and **well drained**. Heavy clay and dry soils are tolerated. Reed grass may be susceptible to rust in cool, wet summers or in areas with poor air circulation. Rain and heavy snow may cause it to flop temporarily, but it quickly bounces back. Cut it back to 2–4" in very early spring before growth begins, and divide it when it begins to die out in the center.

Features: open habit becomes upright; silvery pink flowers turn rich tan; green foliage turns bright gold in fall; winter interest
Height: 3–5' **Spread:** 24–36"
Hardiness: zones 4–9

Tips

Whether it's used as a single, stately focal point, in small groupings or in large drifts, this desirable, low-maintenance grass combines well with late-summer and fall-blooming perennials.

Recommended

C. x *acutiflora* 'Karl Foerster' (Foerster's feather reed grass), the most popular selection, forms a loose mound of green foliage from which airy bottlebrush flowers emerge in June. The flowering stems have a loose, arching habit when they first emerge but grow more stiff and upright over summer. Other cultivars include **'Avalanche,'** a new introduction which has a white center stripe, and **'Overdam,'** a compact, less hardy selection with white leaf edges.

Russian Sage
Perovskia

P. atriplicifolia (above), *P. atriplicifolia* 'Filigran' (below)

Russian sage offers four-season interest in the garden: soft, gray-green leaves on light gray stems in spring; fuzzy, violet-blue flowers in summer; and silvery white stems in fall that last until late winter.

Growing

Russian sage prefers **full sun**. The soil should be **poor to moderately fertile** and **well drained**. Too much water and nitrogen will cause this plant's growth to flop, so do not plant it

Russian sage blossoms make a lovely addition to fresh bouquets and dried-flower arrangements.

next to heavy feeders. Russian sage cannot be divided because it is a subshrub that originates from a single stem.

When new growth appears low on the branches in spring, or in autumn, cut the plant back hard to about 6–12" to encourage vigorous, bushy growth.

Tips

The silvery foliage and blue flowers work well with other plants in the back of a mixed border and soften the appearance of daylilies. Russian sage can also create a soft screen in a natural garden or on a dry bank.

Recommended

P. atriplicifolia is a loose, upright plant with silvery white, finely divided foliage. The small, lavender blue flowers are loosely held on silvery, branched stems. Cultivars are available.

Features: blue or purple mid-summer to autumn flowers; attractive habit; fragrant gray-green foliage **Height:** 3–4'
Spread: 3–4' **Hardiness:** zones 4–9

Sea Holly
Erygium

Sea hollies add structure to the garden with their silvery blue flowers and angular growth habit.

Growing

Sea hollies grow best in **full sun**. The soil should be **average to fertile** and **well drained**. These plants have a long taproot and are fairly drought tolerant, though they grow best if not left dry for too long. They are tolerant of seaside conditions. Avoid dividing because these plants resent having their roots disturbed.

Tips

Mix sea hollies with other late-season bloomers in a border. They make an interesting addition to naturalized gardens.

Wear gloves when handling these plants as the leaves and flower bracts are spiny.

Recommended.

E. alpinum (alpine sea holly) grows 2–4' tall and bears steel blue or white flowers. Cultivars are available.

E. giganteum (giant sea holly) grows 4–5' tall. The steel blue flowers have silvery gray bracts.

E. x tripartium grows 24–36" tall with purple flowers.

E. yuccifolium (rattlesnake master) is native to central and eastern North America. It grows 3–4' tall and bears creamy green to pale blue flowers with gray-green bracts.

Features: attractive stems and foliage; blue, purple, white flowers **Height:** 1–5'
Spread: 12–24" **Hardiness:** zones 4–8

E. giganteum (above), E. x tripartium (below)

The steel blue, globe-shaped flowerheads come in a variety of sizes and are prized for use in fresh or dried flower arrangements. Long lasting but short stemmed, these distinctive blooms are often mounted on florists' wire.

Sea Oats
Chasmanthium

C. latifolium (above & below)

This native grass is at home in moist, shady woodlands, but its bamboo-like foliage gives it a tropical flair.

Growing

Sea oats thrive in **full shade to full sun**, though it must stay moist in full sun to avoid leaf scorch. The upright, cascading habit relaxes in deep shade. The soil should be **fertile** and **moist**, but dry soils are tolerated.

Sea oats vigorously self-seed, but the seedlings are easily removed and composted or shared with friends. Divide to control the rapid spread. Cut this plant back each spring to 2" above the ground.

Tips

Sea oats are tremendous plants for moist, shady areas. Their upright to cascading habit, when in full bloom, makes an attractive planting alongside a stream or pond, in a large drift or in a container. These plants can become invasive in the garden when growing conditions are good.

Recommended

C. latifolium forms a spreading clump of unique, bright green, bamboo-like foliage. The scaly, dangling spikelet flowers arrange themselves nicely on delicate stems just slightly above the foliage. The foliage turns bronze and the flowers turn gold in fall.

Also called: northern sea oats
Features: bamboo-like foliage; unusual flowers; winter interest **Height:** 32"–4'
Spread: 18–24" **Hardiness:** zones 5–9

Sedum

Sedum

Some 300 to 500 species of sedum are distributed throughout the Northern Hemisphere. Many sedums are grown for their foliage, which can range in color from steel gray-blue and green to red and burgundy.

Growing

Sedums prefer **full sun** but tolerate partial shade. The soil should be of **average fertility,** very **well drained** and **neutral to alkaline**. Divide in spring when needed.

Tips

Low-growing sedums make wonderful groundcovers and additions to rock gardens or rock walls. They also edge beds and borders beautifully. Taller sedums give a lovely late-season display in a bed or border.

Recommended

S. acre (gold moss stonecrop) is a low-growing, wide-spreading plant that bears small, yellow-green flowers. It can spread aggressively.

S. **'Autumn Joy'** (autumn joy sedum) is a popular upright hybrid. The flowers open pink or red and later fade to deep bronze.

S. spectabile (showy stonecrop) is an upright species with pink flowers. Cultivars are available.

S. spurium (two-row stonecrop) forms a low, wide mat of foliage with deep pink or white flowers. Many cultivars are available and are often grown for their colorful foliage.

Also called: stonecrop
Features: yellow, white, red, pink summer to autumn flowers; decorative, fleshy foliage
Height: 2–24" **Spread:** 12–24" or more
Hardiness: zones 3–8

S. 'Autumn Joy' (above & below)

Early-summer pruning of upright species and hybrids encourages compact, bushy growth but can delay flowering.

Sensitive Fern

Onoclea

O. sensibilis (above & below)

A common sight along stream banks and in wooded areas, this native fern thrives in moist and shaded conditions.

Growing

Sensitive fern grows best in **light shade** but tolerates full or partial shade. The fronds can scorch if exposed to too much sun. The soil should be **fertile, humus rich** and **moist**, though some drought is tolerated. These plants are sensitive to frost and can be easily damaged by late and early frosts.

Tips

Sensitive ferns like to live in damp, shady places. Include them in shaded borders, woodland gardens and other locations with protection from the wind.

Recommended

O. sensibilis forms a mass of light green, deeply lobed, arching fronds. Fertile fronds are produced in late summer and persist through winter. The spores are produced in structures that look like black beads, and this gives the fertile fronds a decorative appearance that makes them a popular addition to floral arrangements.

These ferns are reputed to tolerate the toxins produced by the black walnut (Julgans nigra), making them a good choice for planting beneath these trees.

Features: deciduous perennial fern; attractive foliage; habit **Height:** 24" **Spread:** indefinite **Hardiness:** zones 4–9

Sweet Woodruff

Galium

G. odoratum (above & below)

Sweet woodruff is a groundcover with abundant good qualities: attractive, light green foliage that smells like new-mown hay; profuse white spring flowers; and the ability to fill in garden spaces without taking over.

Growing

This plant prefers **partial shade**. It will grow well, but will not bloom well, in full shade. The soil should be **humus rich, slightly acidic** and **evenly moist**. Sweet woodruff competes well with other plant roots and does well where some other groundcovers, like vinca, fail to thrive.

Tips

Sweet woodruff makes a perfect woodland groundcover. It forms a beautiful green carpet and loves the same conditions in which azaleas and rhododendrons thrive. Interplant it with spring bulbs for a fantastic spring display.

Recommended

G. odoratum is a low, spreading groundcover. It bears clusters of star-shaped, white flowers in a flush in late spring, and these continue to appear sporadically through mid-summer.

Features: deciduous perennial groundcover; white late-spring to mid-summer flowers; fragrant foliage; habit **Height:** 12–18"
Spread: indefinite **Hardiness:** zones 3–8

Switch Grass
Panicum

P. virgatum cultivar (above)
P. virgatum 'Heavy Metal' (below)

Switch grass' delicate, airy panicles fill gaps in the garden border and can be cut for fresh or dried arrangements.

A native to the prairie grasslands, switch grass naturalizes equally well in an informal border and a natural meadow.

Growing
Switch grass thrives in **full sun, light shade** or **partial shade**. The soil should be of **average fertility** and **well drained**, though plants adapt to moist or dry soils and tolerate conditions ranging from heavy clay to lighter sandy soil. Cut switch grass back to 2–4" from the ground in early spring. The flower stems may break under heavy, wet snow or in exposed, windy sites.

Tips
Plant switch grass singly in small gardens, in large groups in spacious borders or at the edges of ponds or pools for a dramatic, whimsical effect. The seedheads attract birds, and the foliage changes color in the fall, so place this plant where you can enjoy both features.

Recommended
P. virgatum (switch grass) is suited to wild meadow gardens. Some of its popular cultivars include '**Heavy Metal**' (blue switch grass), an upright plant with narrow, steely blue foliage flushed with gold and burgundy in fall; '**Prairie Sky**' (blue switch grass), an arching plant with deep blue foliage; and '**Shenandoah**' (red switch grass), with red-tinged, green foliage that turns burgundy in fall.

Features: clumping habit; green, blue, burgundy foliage; airy panicles of flowers; fall color; winter interest **Height:** 3–5'
Spread: 30–36" **Hardiness:** zones 3–9

Thrift
Armeria

These tough plants form cushion-like mounds from which lollipop-like flowers emerge.

Growing

Thrift grows best in **full sun**. The soil should be of **poor to average fertility, sandy** and **well drained**. It is drought tolerant once established.

Prompt deadheading prolongs the flowering period. Excess fertilizer will reduce flowering and can eventually kill the plant.

Tips

Thrift is a useful plant for rock gardens or the front of the border. It is tolerant of seaside conditions and grows well in coastal gardens. Cut the plant back if it seems to be thinning in the middle, to encourage new growth.

Recommended

A. **Bees' Hybrids** is a group of large hybrids that grow 18–24" tall. The large, showy, pink, white or red flowers are borne in spring and summer.

A. **maritima** forms a clump of grassy foliage. Ball-like clusters of pink, white or purple flowers are borne at the ends of long stems in late spring and early summer. The plant grows up to 8" tall. Cultivars are available, including **'Alba,'** with white flowers, and **'Rubrifolia,'** with burgundy leaves.

A. maritima 'Alba' (above), A. maritima (below)

It has been suggested that this plant is called thrift because it has one root supporting many stalks, so it is 'thrifty' with its roots.

Also called: sea pink, sea thrift
Features: pink, white, red, purple late-spring and summer flowers; habit; foliage
Height: 8–24" **Spread:** 12–24"
Hardiness: zones 3–8

Vinca
Vinca

V inca grows well in a wide range of soils and welcomes spring with a bounty of blue flowers.

Growing

Vinca grows well in **partial to full shade**. **Moist, well-drained** soil of any type will do. After planting, mulch the soil with shredded leaves and compost to keep the soil moist and to prevent weeds from sprouting up while vinca fills in.

Tips

Vinca is a useful and attractive groundcover in a shrub border, under trees or on a shady bank. Vinca is shallow-rooted and can out-compete weeds without interfering with deeper-rooted shrubs. Shear plants back in early spring if they begin to outgrow their space.

Recommended

V. minor forms a low, loose mat of trailing stems. Purple or blue flowers are borne in a flush in spring and sporadically throughout summer. Many cultivars are available, with different-colored flowers or variegated foliage.

V. minor (above & below)

The Romans used the long, trailing stems of vinca to make wreaths. This use of the plant may explain its name, which is derived from the Latin vincire, *'to bind.'*

Also called: myrtle, lesser periwinkle
Features: blue, purple, white, red mid-spring to fall flowers; trailing habit **Height:** 4–8"
Spread: indefinite **Hardiness:** zones 4–8

Yarrow
Achillea

*Y*arrows are informal, tough plants with a fantastic color range.

Growing

Yarrows grow best in **full sun**. The soil should be of **average fertility, sandy** and **well drained**. These plants tolerate drought and poor soil. They also tolerate heavy, wet soil and humidity, but they do not thrive in such conditions. Excessively rich soil or too much nitrogen results in weak, floppy growth. Divide every two or three years in spring.

Deadhead to prolong blooming. Basal foliage should be left in place over the winter and tidied up in spring.

Tips

Cottage gardens, wildflower gardens and mixed borders are perfect places for these informal plants. They thrive in hot, dry locations where nothing else will grow.

Yarrows make excellent groundcovers. They send up shoots and flowers from a low basal point and may be mowed periodically without excessive damage to the plant. Mower blades should be kept at least 4" high.

Recommended

A. filipendulina forms a clump of ferny foliage and bears yellow flowers. It has been used to develop several hybrids and cultivars.

A. millefolium 'Paprika' (above)
A. millefolium 'Summer Pastels' (below)

*A. **millefolium*** (common yarrow) forms a clump of soft, finely divided foliage and bears white flowers. Many cultivars exist, with flowers in a wide range of colors.

Features: white, yellow, red, orange, pink, purple mid-summer to early-autumn flowers; attractive foliage; spreading habit
Height: 4"–4'   **Spread:** 12–36"
Hardiness: zones 3–9

Bayberry
Myrica

M. pensylvanica

Bayberry is a wonderful shrub that can stand alone as a specimen or blend easily into a mixed border.

Growing

Bayberry grows well in **full sun** or **partial shade**. It adapts to most soil conditions, from poor, sandy soil to heavy clay soil. Bayberry tolerates salty conditions, making it useful where coastal conditions or winter road spray may kill less tolerant plants. It rarely needs any pruning.

Tips

This adaptable plant forms large colonies and can be used for mass plantings in underused areas and in seaside gardens. Single plants can be included in borders or used as specimens.

Recommended

M. pensylvanica is a dense, rounded, suckering shrub. Insignificant flowers are borne in early to mid-spring. Male and female flowers are generally produced on separate plants, and both are required for a good show of fruit on the female. Small, waxy, gray fruit persist through winter.

The waxy fruit of this eastern North American native is used in candle making.

Features: aromatic, deciduous to semi-evergreen shrub; foliage; dense, suckering habit; persistent fruit **Height:** 5–12' **Spread:** 5–12' **Hardiness:** zones 3–6

Beech
Fagus

F. sylvatica 'Pendula' (above), *F. sylvatica* (below)

The aristocrats of the large shade trees, the majestic beeches are attractive at any age, from their big, bold, beautiful youth through to their slow, craggy decline.

Growing
Beeches grow equally well in **full sun** or **partial shade**. The soil should be of **average fertility, loamy** and **well drained**, though almost all well-drained soils are tolerated.

American beech doesn't like having its roots disturbed and should be transplanted only when very young. European beech transplants easily and is more tolerant of varied soil conditions than is American beech.

Tips
Beeches make excellent specimens. They are also used as shade trees and in woodland gardens. These trees need a lot of space, but the European beech's adaptability to pruning makes it a reasonable choice in a small garden if you are willing and able to prune it.

Recommended
F. grandifolia (American beech) is a broad-canopied tree native to most of eastern North America.

F. sylvatica (European beech) is a spectacular broad tree with a number of interesting cultivars. Several are small enough to use in the home garden. There are narrow, columnar or weeping varieties and varieties with purple, yellow or pink, white and green variegated foliage.

The nuts of the beech tree are edible when roasted.

Features: large, oval, deciduous shade tree; foliage; bark; habit; fall color; fruit
Height: 30–80' **Spread:** 10–65'
Hardiness: zones 4–9

Butterfly Bush
Buddleia

B. davidii (above & below)

Butterfly bushes are among the best shrubs for attracting butterflies and bees to your garden, so avoid spraying your plant for pests—you will harm the beautiful and beneficial insects that make their homes there.

This attractive bush with its fragrant flowers will attract countless butterflies along with a wide variety of other pollinating insects.

Growing
Butterfly bushes prefer to grow in **full sun**, producing few if any flowers in shady conditions. The soil should be **fertile to average** and **well drained**. Plants are drought tolerant once established. Plants flower on the current year's growth, so even if plants are killed back over the winter, they will still produce blooms.

Tips
Butterfly bushes make beautiful additions to shrub and mixed borders. The graceful arching habit makes them ideal as specimen plants. The dwarf forms that stay under 5' are suitable for small gardens.

Recommended
B. davidii (orange-eye butterfly bush, summer lilac) is the most commonly grown species. It grows 4–10' tall, with an equal spread. It bears fragrant flowers in bright and pastel shades of purple, pink, blue or white from mid-summer through fall. Many cultivars are available.

B. x *weyeriana* is a wide-spreading shrub with arching stems. It grows 6–12' tall, spreads 5–10' and bears purple or yellow flowers from mid-summer through fall. Cultivars are available. (Zones 6–9)

Features: large, deciduous shrub with arching branches and attractive flowers, habit and foliage **Height:** 4–12' **Spread:** 4–10' **Hardiness:** zones 5–9

Caryopteris
Caryopteris

Caryopteris is cultivated for its aromatic stems, foliage and flowers. A few cut stems in a vase will delicately scent a room.

Growing
Caryopteris prefers **full sun**, but it tolerates light shade. It does best in soil of **average fertility** that is **light** and **well drained**. Wet and poorly drained soils can kill this plant. Caryopteris is very drought tolerant once established. Treat it as a herbaceous perennial if growth is regularly killed back over the winter.

Tips
Include caryopteris in your shrub or mixed border. The bright blue, late-season flowers are welcome when many other plants are past their flowering best.

Recommended
C. x *clandonensis* forms a dense mound that grows up to 3' tall and 3–5' in spread. It bears clusters of blue or purple flowers in late summer and early fall. Cultivars are available and are more often grown than the species.

C. x *clandonensis* 'Dark Knight' (above), C. x *clandonensis* (below)

Caryopteris is sometimes killed back over cold winters. Cut back the dead growth in spring. New shoots will sprout from the base, providing you with plenty of late-summer flowers.

Also called: bluebeard, blue spirea
Features: rounded, spreading, deciduous shrub with attractive, fragrant foliage, twigs and late-summer flowers **Height:** 2–4'
Spread: 2–5' **Hardiness:** zones 5–9

Cedar
Thuja

T. occidentalis 'Little Gem' (above)
T. occidentalis (below)

Deer enjoy eating the foliage of eastern arborvitae. Use western arborvitae, which is relatively resistant to deer browsing, instead.

Cedars are rot resistant, durable and long lived, earning quiet admiration from gardeners everywhere.

Growing

Cedars prefer **full sun** but tolerate light to partial shade. The soil should be of **average fertility, moist** and **well drained**. These plants enjoy humidity and in the wild are often found growing near marshy areas. Cedars will perform best in a location with some shelter from wind, especially in winter, when the foliage can easily dry out and give the entire plant a rather brown, drab appearance.

Tips

Large varieties of cedar make excellent specimen trees, and smaller cultivars can be used in foundation plantings and shrub borders and as formal or informal hedges.

Recommended

T. occidentalis (eastern arborvitae, eastern white cedar) is a narrow, pyramidal tree with scale-like, evergreen needles. There are dozens of cultivars available, including shrubby dwarf varieties, varieties with yellow foliage and smaller, upright varieties. (Zones 2–7; cultivars may be less cold hardy)

T. plicata (western arborvitae, western redcedar) is a narrowly pyramidal, evergreen tree that grows quickly, resists deer browsing and maintains good foliage color all winter. Several cultivars are available, including several dwarf varieties and a yellow and green variegated variety. (Zones 5–9)

Also called: arborvitae **Features:** small to large, evergreen shrub or tree; foliage; bark; form **Height:** 2–50' **Spread:** 2–20' **Hardiness:** zones 2–9

Cotoneaster
Cotoneaster

C. apiculatus (above), *C. dammeri* (below)

With their diverse sizes, shapes, flowers, fruit and foliage, cotoneasters are so versatile that they border on being overused.

Growing

Cotoneasters grow well in **full sun** or **partial shade**. The soil should be of **average fertility** and **well drained**.

Tips

Cotoneasters can be included in shrub or mixed borders. Low spreaders work well as groundcover, and shrubby species can be used to form hedges. Larger species are grown as small specimen trees, and some low growers are grafted onto standards and grown as small, weeping trees.

Features: evergreen or deciduous, groundcover, shrub or small tree; foliage; early-summer flowers; persistent fruit; variety of forms **Height:** 6"–15' **Spread:** 3–12' **Hardiness:** zones 4–9

Recommended

There are many cotoneasters to choose from. *C. adpressus* (creeping cotoneaster), *C.* x **'Hessei'** and *C. horizontalis* (rockspray cotoneaster) are low-growing, groundcover plants. Species such as *C. apiculatus* (cranberry cotoneaster) and *C. dammeri* (bearberry cotoneaster) are wide-spreading, low and shrubby plants. *C. salicifolius* (willowleaf cotoneaster) is an upright, shrubby plant that can be trained to form a small tree. These are just a few possibilities; your local garden center can help you choose a plant to suit your garden.

Crabapple

Malus

Pure white through deep pink flowers, heights between 5' and 30' with similar spreads, tolerance of winter's extreme cold and summer's baking heat and yellow through candy apple red fruit often persisting through winter—what more could anyone ask from a tree?

Growing

Crabapples prefer **full sun** but tolerate partial shade. The soil should be of **average to rich fertility, moist** and **well drained**. These trees tolerate damp soil.

One of the best ways to prevent the spread of crabapple pests and diseases is to clean up all the leaves and fruit that fall off the tree. Many pests overwinter in the fruit, leaves or soil at the base of the tree. Clearing away their winter shelter helps keep populations under control.

Tips

Crabapples make excellent specimen plants. Many varieties are quite small, so there is one to suit almost any size of garden. Some forms are even small enough to grow in large containers. Crabapples' flexible, young branches make them good choices for creating espalier specimens along a wall or fence.

Recommended

There are hundreds of crabapples available. When choosing a species, variety or cultivar, one of the most important attributes to look for is disease resistance. Even the most beautiful flowers, fruit or habit will never look good if the plant is ravaged by pests or disease. Ask for information about new, resistant cultivars at your local nursery or garden center.

Features: rounded, mounded or spreading, small to medium deciduous tree; spring flowers; late-season and winter fruit; fall foliage; habit; bark **Height:** 5–30' **Spread:** 6–30' **Hardiness:** zones 4–8

Dogwood
Cornus

S tem color, leaf variegation, fall color, growth habit, soil adaptability and hardiness are all positive attributes to be found in dogwoods.

Growing

Dogwoods grow equally well in **full sun, light shade** or **partial shade**, with a slight preference for light shade. The soil should be of **average to high fertility, high in organic matter, neutral or slightly acidic** and **well drained**.

Tips

Shrub dogwoods can be included in a shrub or mixed border. They look best in groups rather than as single specimens. The tree species make wonderful specimen plants and are small enough to include in most gardens.

Recommended

C. alba (red-twig dogwood, Tartarian dogwood) and *C. sericea* (*C. stolonifera*; red-osier dogwood) have bright red stems that provide winter interest. Cultivars are available with stems in varied shades of red, orange or yellow. Fall foliage color can also be attractive. (Zones 2–7)

C. alternifolia (pagoda dogwood) can be grown as a large, multi-stemmed shrub or a small, single-stemmed tree. The branches have an attractive layered appearance. Clusters of small, white flowers appear in early summer. (Zones 3–8)

C. alba 'Bailhalo' (above), *C. kousa* var. *chinensis* (below)

C. kousa (Kousa dogwood) is grown for its flowers, fruit, fall color and interesting bark. The white-bracted flowers are followed by bright red fruit. The foliage turns red and purple in fall. **Var.** *chinensis* (Chinese dogwood) grows more vigorously and has larger flowers. (Zones 5–9)

Features: deciduous, large shrub or small tree; late-spring to early-summer flowers; fall foliage; stem color; fruit; habit **Height:** 5–30' **Spread:** 5–30' **Hardiness:** zones 2–9

Elder
Sambucus

S. racemosa (above & below)

Elders work well in a naturalized garden. Cultivars are available that provide light texture in a dark area, dark foliage in a bright area or variegated yellow foliage and bright stems in brilliant sunshine.

Growing

Elders grow well in **full sun** or **partial shade**. Cultivars and varieties grown for interesting leaf color develop the best color in light or partial shade. The soil should be of **average fertility, moist** and **well drained**. These plants tolerate dry soil once established.

Tips

Elders can be used in a shrub or mixed border, in a natural woodland garden or next to a pond or other water feature. Types with interesting or colorful foliage can be used as specimen plants or focal points.

Recommended

S. canadensis (American elder/elderberry), *S. nigra* (European elder/elderberry, black elder/elderberry) and *S. racemosa* (European red elder/elderberry) are rounded shrubs with white or pinkish white flowers followed by red or dark purple berries. Cultivars are available with green, yellow, bronze or purple foliage and deeply divided feathery foliage.

Also called: elderberry **Features:** large, bushy, deciduous shrub; early-summer flowers; fruit; foliage **Height:** 5–20' **Spread:** 5–20' **Hardiness:** zones 3–9

Enkianthus
Enkianthus

Enkianthus is one of the best shrubs for adding stunning fall color to your garden.

Growing
Enkianthus grows well in **full sun, partial shade** or **light shade**. The soil should be **fertile, humus rich, moist, acidic** and **well drained**.

Tips
Enkianthus is a beautiful shrub to include in the understory of a woodland garden and can be used in a mixed border or as a specimen plant. It also makes an excellent companion for rhododendrons and other acid-loving plants.

Recommended
E. campanulatus (red-vein enkianthus) is a large, bushy shrub or small tree that grows 10–15' tall, with an equal spread. It bears clusters of small, white, red-veined, pendulous, bell-shaped flowers in spring. The foliage turns fantastic shades of yellow, orange and red in fall. (Zones 4–7)

E. perulatus (white enkianthus) is a compact shrub that grows 5–6' tall, with an equal spread. It produces white flowers in mid-spring. The foliage turns bright red in fall. (Zones 5–8)

E. campanulatus (above & below)

The layered branching and tufted foliage of enkianthus will add a unique touch to your garden.

Features: bushy, deciduous shrub or small tree; spring flowers; fall foliage
Height: 5–15' **Spread:** 5–15'
Hardiness: zones 4–8

Euonymus
Euonymus

uonymus, with its interesting leaf colorings and plant habits, has many uses.

Growing

Euonymus species prefer **full sun** but tolerate light or partial shade. Soil of **average to rich fertility** is preferable, but any **moist, well-drained** soil will do.

Tips

E. fortunei can be grown as a shrub in borders or as a hedge. It is an excellent substitute for the more demanding boxwood. The trailing habit also makes it useful as a groundcover or climber.

Recommended

E. fortunei (wintercreeper euonymus) as a species is rarely grown owing to the wide and attractive variety of cultivars. These can be prostrate, climbing or mounding evergreens, often with attractive, variegated foliage.

E. fortunei 'Emerald 'n' Gold' (above & below)

Burning bush or winged euonymus (E. alatus) is another common species of euonymus. It is considered invasive in both Massachusetts and New Hampshire and is no longer recommended in New England gardens.

Features: evergreen shrub, groundcover or climber; foliage; habit **Height:** 18"–20'
Spread: 18"–20' **Hardiness:** zones 3–9

False Cypress
Chamaecyparis

Conifer shoppers are blessed with a marvelous selection of false cypresses that offer color, size, shape and growth habits not available in most other evergreens.

Growing

False cypresses prefer **full sun**. The soil should be **fertile, moist, neutral to acidic** and **well drained**. Alkaline soils are tolerated. In shaded areas, growth may be sparse or thin.

Tips

Tree varieties are used as specimen plants and for hedging. The dwarf and slow-growing cultivars are used in borders and rock gardens and as bonsai. False cypress shrubs can be grown near the house or as evergreen specimens in large containers.

Recommended

There are several available species of false cypress and many cultivars. The scaly foliage can be in a drooping or strand form, in fan-like or feathery sprays and may be dark green, bright green or yellow. Plant forms vary too, from mounding or rounded to tall and pyramidal or narrow with pendulous branches. Check with your local garden center or nursery to see what is available.

The oils in the foliage of false cypresses may irritate sensitive skin.

C. pisifera 'Mops' (above)
C. nootkatensis 'Pendula' (below)

Features: narrow, pyramidal, evergreen tree or shrub; cultivars vary; foliage; habit; cones
Height: 18"–150' **Spread:** 18'–80'
Hardiness: zones 4–8

Flowering Cherry, Plum & Almond

Prunus

P. sargentii (above)

Cherries are so beautiful and uplifting after the gray days of winter that few gardeners can resist them.

Growing

These flowering fruit trees prefer **full sun**. The soil should be of **average fertility, moist** and **well drained**. Shallow roots will emerge from the lawn if the tree is not getting sufficient water.

Tips

Prunus species are beautiful as specimen plants and many are small enough for almost any garden. Small species and cultivars can be included in borders or grouped to form informal hedges or barriers. Pissard plum and purpleleaf sand cherry can be trained to form formal hedges.

Because of the pest problems that afflict many of the cherries, they can be rather short-lived. Choose resistant species such as Sargent cherry. If you plant a more susceptible species, such as the Japanese flowering cherry, enjoy it while it thrives but be prepared to replace it if problems become severe.

Recommended

Following are a few popular selections from the many species, hybrids and cultivars available. Check with your local nursery or garden center for other possible selections. *P. cerasifera* 'Atropurpurea' (Pissard plum) and *P.* x *cistena* (purpleleaf sand cherry) are shrubby plants with purple foliage and light pink flowers. *P. sargentii* (Sargent cherry) and *P. serrulata* (Japanese flowering cherry) are rounded or spreading trees grown for their white or light pink flowers, often-attractive bark and bright fall color.

Features: upright, rounded, spreading or weeping, deciduous tree or shrub; spring to early-summer flowers; fruit; bark; fall foliage
Height: 4–75' **Spread:** 4–50'
Hardiness: zones 4–8

Fothergilla

Fothergilla

Flowers, fragrance, fall color and interesting, soft tan to brownish stems give fothergillas year-round appeal.

Growing

Fothergillas grow equally well in **full sun** or **partial shade**. In full sun these plants bear the most flowers and have the best fall color. The soil should be of **average fertility, acidic, humus rich, moist** and **well drained**.

Tips

Fothergillas are attractive and useful in shrub or mixed borders, in woodland gardens and when combined with evergreen groundcover.

Recommended

Cultivars are available for both species.

F. gardenii (dwarf fothergilla) is a bushy shrub that bears fragrant, white flowers. The foliage turns yellow, orange and red in fall.

F. major (large fothergilla) is a larger, rounded shrub that bears fragrant, white flowers. The fall foliage colors are yellow, orange and scarlet.

F. major (above & below)

The bottlebrush-shaped spring flowers of fothergillas have a delicate honey scent.

Features: dense, rounded or bushy, deciduous shrub; spring flowers; scent; fall foliage **Height:** 2–10'
Spread: 2–10' **Hardiness:** zones 4–9

Fringe Tree
Chionanthus

C. virginicus (above & below)

Fringe trees adapt to a wide range of growing conditions, are cold hardy and are densely covered in silky white, honey-scented flowers that shimmer in the wind over a long period in spring.

Growing
Fringe trees prefer **full sun**. They do best in soil that is **fertile, acidic, moist** and **well drained** but adapt to most soil conditions. In the wild they are often found growing alongside stream banks.

Tips
Fringe trees work well as specimen plants, as part of a border or beside a water feature. Plants begin flowering at a very early age.

Fringe trees can be very difficult to find in general nurseries. On-line nurseries and plant sales at botanical gardens, universities or colleges are the most likely places to find them.

Recommended
C. retusus (Chinese fringe tree) is a rounded, spreading shrub or small tree with deeply furrowed, peeling bark and erect, fragrant, white flower clusters. (Zones 5–8)

C. virginicus (white fringe tree) is a spreading small tree or large shrub that bears drooping, fragrant, white flowers. (Zones 4–8)

Features: rounded or spreading, deciduous, large shrub or small tree; early-summer flowers; bark; habit **Height:** 10–25' **Spread:** 10–25' **Hardiness:** zones 4–9

Hawthorn
Crataegus

The hawthorns are uncommonly beautiful trees. In spring they provide a generous show of beautiful, apple-like blossoms, and in fall they bear persistent, glossy red fruit and often have colorful foliage.

Growing

Hawthorns grow equally well in **full sun** or **partial shade**. They adapt to any **well-drained** soil and tolerate urban conditions.

Tips

Hawthorns can be grown as specimen plants or hedges in urban sites, lakeside gardens and exposed locations. They are popular in areas where vandalism is a problem because very few people wish to grapple with plants bearing stiff, 2" long thorns. As a hedge, hawthorns create an almost impenetrable barrier.

These trees are small enough to include in most gardens. With their long, sharp thorns, however, hawthorns might not be good selections where there are children about.

Recommended

C. laevigata (*C. oxycantha*; English hawthorn) is a low-branching, rounded tree with zigzag layers of thorny branches. It bears white or pink flowers, followed by red fruit in late summer. Many cultivars are available.

C. phaenopyrum (above), *C. laevigata* 'Paul's Scarlet' (below)

C. phaenopyrum (*C. cordata*; Washington hawthorn) is an oval to rounded, thorny tree. In fall, the glossy green foliage turns red and orange, and the white flowers become persistent, shiny red fruit.

Features: rounded, deciduous tree, often with a zigzagged, layered branch pattern; late-spring or early-summer flowers; fruit; foliage; thorny branches **Height:** 15–35' **Spread:** 12–35' **Hardiness:** zones 3–8

Hemlock
Tsuga

T. canadensis 'Jeddeloh' (above), *T. canadensis* (below)

Many people would agree that eastern hemlock is one of the most beautiful, graceful evergreen trees in the world. The movement, softness and agility of this tree make it easy to place in the landscape.

Growing
Hemlock generally grows well in any light from **full sun to full shade**. The soil should be **humus rich, moist** and **well drained**. Hemlock is drought sensitive and grows best in

cool, moist conditions. It is also sensitive to air pollution and suffers salt damage, so keep hemlock away from roadways.

Tips
This elegant tree, with its delicate needles, is one of the most beautiful evergreens to use as a specimen tree. Hemlock can be pruned to keep it within bounds or shaped to form a hedge. The smaller cultivars may be included in a shrub or mixed border. The many dwarf forms are useful in smaller gardens.

Recommended
T. canadensis (eastern hemlock, Canadian hemlock) is a graceful, narrowly pyramidal tree. Many cultivars are available, including groundcover, pendulous and dwarf forms.

Features: pyramidal or columnar, evergreen tree or shrub; foliage; habit; cones
Height: 18"–80' **Spread:** 18"–35'
Hardiness: zones 3–8

Holly
Ilex

ollies vary greatly in shape and size and can be such delights when placed with full consideration for their needs.

Growing
These plants prefer **full sun** but tolerate partial shade. The soil should be of **average to rich fertility, humus rich** and **moist**. Hollies perform best in **acidic** soil with a pH of 6.5–6.0 or lower. Shelter hollies from winter wind to help prevent the evergreen leaves from drying out. Apply a summer mulch to keep the roots cool and moist.

Tips
Hollies can be used in groups, in woodland gardens and in shrub and mixed borders. They can also be shaped into hedges. Winterberry is good for naturalizing in moist sites.

Recommended
I. glabra (inkberry) is a rounded shrub with glossy, deep green, evergreen foliage and dark purple fruit. Cultivars are available. (Zones 4–9)

I. x meserveae (meserve holly, blue holly) is a group of hybrids that originated from crosses between tender English holly (*I. aquifolium*) and hardy hollies like prostrate holly (*I. rugosa*). These dense, evergreen shrubs may be erect, mounding or spreading. (Zones 5–8)

I. x meserveae hybrid (above), *I. x meserveae* 'Blue Girl' (below)

I. verticillata (winterberry, winterberry holly) is a deciduous native species grown for its explosion of red fruit that persists into winter. Many cultivars and hybrids are available. (Zones 3–9)

Also called: inkberry, winterberry
Features: erect or spreading, evergreen or deciduous shrub or tree; glossy, sometimes spiny foliage; fruit, habit **Height:** 3–50'
Spread: 3–40' **Hardiness:** zones 3–9

Horsechestnut

Aesculus

A. parviflora (above), A. hippocastanum (below)

These trees provide heavy shade, which is excellent for cooling buildings but makes it difficult to grow grass beneath the trees.

Horsechestnuts range from trees with immense regal bearing to small but impressive shrubs. All have spectacular flowers.

Growing

Horsechestnuts grow well in **full sun** or **partial shade**. The soil should be **fertile, moist** and **well drained**. These trees dislike excessive drought.

Tips

Horsechestnuts are used as specimen and shade trees. The roots of horsechestnuts can break up sidewalks and patios if planted too close.

The smaller, shrubby horsechestnuts grow well near pond plantings and also make interesting specimens. Give them plenty of space as they can form large colonies.

Recommended

A. hippocastanum (common horsechestnut) is a large, rounded tree that will branch right to the ground if grown in an open setting. The flowers, white with yellow or pink marks, are borne in long spikes. (Zones 3–7)

A. parviflora (bottlebrush buckeye) is a spreading, mound-forming, suckering shrub that has plentiful spikes of creamy white flowers. (Zones 4–9)

A. pavia (red buckeye) is a low-growing to rounded shrubby tree with cherry red flowers and handsome foliage. It needs consistent moisture. (Zones 4–8)

Also called: buckeye **Features:** rounded or spreading, deciduous tree or shrub; early-summer flowers; foliage; spiny fruit **Height:** 8–80' **Spread:** 8–65' **Hardiness:** zones 3–9

Hydrangea
Hydrangea

ydrangeas have many attractive qualities, including showy, often long-lasting flowers and glossy green leaves, some of which develop beautiful colors in fall.

H. quercifolia (above), H. paniculata 'Grandiflora' (below)

Growing

Hydrangeas grow well in **full sun** or **partial shade**. Some species tolerate full shade. Shade or partial shade reduces leaf and flower scorch in hotter gardens. The soil should be of **average to high fertility, humus rich, moist** and **well drained**. These plants perform best in cool, moist conditions. They need lots of water.

Tips

Hydrangeas can be included in shrub or mixed borders, used as specimens or informal barriers and planted in groups or containers.

Recommended

H. arborescens (smooth hydrangea) is a rounded shrub that flowers well, even in shade. It is rarely grown in favor of the cultivars that bear large clusters of white blossoms. (Zones 3–9)

H. macrophylla (bigleaf hydrangea) is a rounded shrub that bears pink, red, blue or purple flowers from mid- to late summer. Many cultivars are available, including ENDLESS SUMMER, which blooms on both old and new growth. (Zones 5–9)

H. paniculata (panicle hydrangea) is a spreading to upright large shrub or small tree that bears white flowers from late summer to early fall. **'Grandiflora'** (Peegee hydrangea) is a commonly available cultivar. (Zones 4–8)

H. quercifolia (oakleaf hydrangea) is a mound-forming shrub with cinnamon brown, exfoliating bark, conical clusters of sterile and fertile flowers, and large leaves that are lobed like an oak's and turn bronze to bright red in fall. Cultivars are available. (Zones 4–8)

Features: deciduous, mounding or spreading shrub or tree; flowers; habit; foliage; bark
Height: 3–20' **Spread:** 3–10'
Hardiness: zones 3–9

Juniper
Juniperus

J. horizontalis 'Blue Chip' (above), *J. horizontalis* 'Blue Prince' (below)

With all the choices available, from low, creeping plants to upright pyramidal forms, there may be a juniper in every gardener's future,

Growing

Junipers prefer **full sun** but tolerate light shade. Ideally, the soil should be of **average fertility** and **well drained**, but these plants tolerate most conditions.

Tips

Junipers have endless uses. They make prickly barriers and hedges, and can be used in borders, as specimens or in groups. The larger species can be used to form windbreaks, while the low-growing species can be used in rock gardens and as groundcovers.

Recommended

Junipers vary, not just from species to species, but often within a species. Cultivars are available for all species and may differ significantly from the species. *J. chinensis* (Chinese juniper) is a conical tree or spreading shrub. *J. horizontalis* (creeping juniper) is a prostrate, creeping groundcover. *J. procumbens* (Japanese garden juniper) is a wide-spreading, stiff-branched, low shrub. *J. scopulorum* (Rocky Mountain juniper) can be upright, rounded, weeping or spreading. *J. squamata* (singleseed juniper) forms a prostrate or low, spreading shrub or a small, upright tree. *J. virginiana* (eastern redcedar) is a durable tree, upright or wide-spreading.

Features: conical or columnar tree, rounded or spreading shrub, prostrate groundcover; evergreen foliage; variety of colors, sizes and habits **Height:** 4"–80' **Spread:** 18"–25' **Hardiness:** zones 3–9

Katsura-Tree

Cercidiphyllum

*T*he katsura-tree is a classic tree that will add distinction and grace to any planting. Even in youth it is poised and elegant, and it is bound to become a bewitching, mature specimen.

Growing

Katsura-tree grows equally well in **full sun** or **partial shade**. The soil should be **fertile, humus rich, neutral to acidic, moist** and **well drained**. This tree will become established more quickly if watered regularly during dry spells for the first year or two.

Tips

Katsura-tree is useful as a specimen or shade tree. The species is quite large and is best used in large gardens. The cultivar 'Pendula' is quite wide-spreading but can be used in smaller gardens.

Recommended

C. japonicum is a slow-growing tree with heart-shaped, blue-green foliage that turns yellow and orange in fall and develops a spicy scent. **'Pendula'** is one of the most elegant weeping trees available. When grafted to a standard, the mounding, cascading branches give the entire tree the appearance of a waterfall tumbling over rocks.

C. japonicum 'Pendula' (above), *C. japonicum* (below)

This tree is native to eastern Asia, and the delicate foliage blends well into Japanese-style gardens.

Features: rounded or spreading, often multi-stemmed, deciduous tree; summer and fall foliage; habit **Height:** 10–65' **Spread:** 10–65' **Hardiness:** zones 4–8

Lilac

Syringa

S. *meyeri* (above), S. *vulgaris* (below)

Growing

Lilacs grow best in **full sun**. The soil should be **fertile, humus rich** and **well drained**. These plants tolerate open, windy locations.

Tips

Include lilacs in a shrub or mixed border, or use them to create an informal hedge. Japanese tree lilac can be used as a specimen tree.

Recommended

S. x *hyacinthiflora* (hyacinth-flowered lilac, early-flowering lilac) is a group of hardy, upright hybrids that become spreading as they mature. Clusters of fragrant flowers appear two weeks earlier than those of the French lilacs. The leaves turn reddish purple in fall. Many cultivars are available. (Zones 3–7)

S. meyeri (Meyer lilac) is a compact, rounded shrub that bears fragrant, pink or lavender flowers. (Zones 3–7)

S. reticulata (Japanese tree lilac) is a rounded, large shrub or small tree that bears white flowers. **'Ivory Silk'** has a more compact habit and produces more flowers than the species. (Zones 3–7)

S. vulgaris (French lilac, common lilac) is the plant most people think of when they think of lilacs. It is a suckering, spreading shrub with an irregular habit that bears fragrant, lilac-colored flowers. Hundreds of cultivars with a variety of flower colors are available. (Zones 3–8)

The hardest thing about growing lilacs is choosing from the many species and hundreds of cultivars available.

Features: rounded or suckering, deciduous shrub or small tree; late-spring to mid-summer flowers; habit **Height:** 3–30' **Spread:** 3–25' **Hardiness:** zones 2–8

Linden

Tilia

*L*indens are picturesque shade trees with a signature gumdrop shape and sweet-scented flowers that capture the essence of summer.

Growing
Lindens grow best in **full sun**. The soil should be **average to fertile, moist** and **well drained**. These trees adapt to most pH levels but prefer an **alkaline** soil. They tolerate pollution and urban conditions.

Tips
Lindens are useful and attractive street, shade and specimen trees. Their tolerance of pollution and their moderate size make lindens ideal for city gardens.

Recommended
T. cordata (littleleaf linden) is a dense, pyramidal tree that may become rounded with age. It bears small, fragrant flowers with narrow, yellow-green bracts. Cultivars are available.

T. tomentosa (silver linden) has a broad pyramidal or rounded habit that bears small, fragrant flowers and has glossy green leaves with fuzzy, silvery undersides.

T. cordata (above)

Given enough space to spread, lindens will branch right to the ground.

Features: dense, pyramidal to rounded, deciduous tree; habit; foliage
Height: 20–65' **Spread:** 15–50'
Hardiness: zones 3–8

Magnolia
Magnolia

M. x soulangeana (above & below)

Many hybrid magnolias have been introduced in recent years, including hardier, later-flowering selections and yellow-flowered selections.

Magnolias are beautiful, fragrant, versatile plants that also provide attractive winter structure.

Growing

Magnolias grow well in **full sun** or **partial shade**. The soil should be **fertile, humus rich, acidic, moist** and **well drained**. A summer mulch will help keep the roots cool and the soil moist.

Tips

Magnolias are used as specimen trees and the smaller species can be used in borders.

Avoid planting magnolias where the morning sun will encourage the blooms to open too early in the season. Cold, wind and rain can damage the blossoms.

Recommended

Many species, hybrids and cultivars, in a range of sizes and with differing flowering times and colors, are available. Look for two of the most common, **M. x soulangeana** (saucer magnolia), a rounded, spreading, deciduous shrub or tree with pink, purple or white flowers; and **M. stellata** (star magnolia), a compact, bushy or spreading, deciduous shrub or small tree with many-petaled, fragrant, white flowers. Check with your local nursery or garden center for other available magnolias.

Features: upright to spreading, deciduous shrub or tree; flowers; fruit; foliage; habit; bark **Height:** 8–40' **Spread:** 5–35' **Hardiness:** zones 3–9

Maple
Acer

Maples are attractive all year, with delicate flowers in spring, attractive foliage and hanging samaras in summer, vibrant leaf color in fall, and interesting bark and branch structures in winter.

Growing

Generally, maples do well in **full sun** or **light shade,** though this varies from species to species. The soil should be **fertile, moist, humus rich** and **well drained**.

Tips

Maples can be used as specimen trees, as large elements in shrub or mixed borders or as hedges. Some are useful as understory plants bordering wooded areas; others can be grown in containers on patios or terraces. Few Japanese gardens are without the attractive smaller maples. Almost all maples can be used to create bonsai specimens.

Recommended

Maples are some of the most popular trees used as shade or street trees. Many are very large when fully mature, but there are also a few smaller species that are useful in smaller gardens, including *A. campestre* (hedge maple), *A. ginnala* (amur maple), *A. palmatum* (Japanese maple) and *A. rubrum* (red maple). Check with your local nursery or garden center for availability.

A. palmatum cultivars (above & below)

Maple wood is hard and dense and is used for fine furniture construction and for some musical instruments.

Features: small, multi-stemmed, deciduous tree or large shrub; foliage; bark; winged fruit; fall color; form; flowers **Height:** 6–80'
Spread: 6–70' **Hardiness:** zones 2–8

Oak
Quercus

Q. alba (above), Q. robur (below)

The oak's classic shape, outstanding fall color, deep roots and long life are some of its many assets. Plant it for its individual beauty and for posterity.

Growing
Oaks grow well in **full sun** or **partial shade**. The soil should be **fertile, moist** and **well drained**. These trees can be difficult to establish; transplant them only while they are young.

Acorns are generally not edible, though certain species acorns can be eaten once they have been processed to leach out the bitter tannins.

Tips
Oaks are large trees that are best as specimens or for groves in parks and large gardens. Do not disturb the ground around the base of an oak; this tree is very sensitive to changes in grade.

Recommended
There are many oaks to choose from. A few popular species are *Q. alba* (white oak), a rounded, spreading tree with peeling bark and purple-red fall color; *Q. coccinea* (scarlet oak), noted for having the most brilliant red fall color of all the oaks; *Q. robur* (English oak), a rounded, spreading tree with golden yellow fall color; and *Q. rubra* (red oak), a rounded, spreading tree with fall color ranging from yellow to red-brown. Some cultivars are available. Check with your local nursery or garden center.

Features: large, rounded, spreading, deciduous tree; summer and fall foliage; bark; habit; acorns **Height:** 35–120' **Spread:** 10–100' **Hardiness:** zones 3–9

Pine
Pinus

P. mugo (above), P. strobus (below)

Pines offer exciting possibilities for any garden. Exotic-looking pines are available with soft or stiff needles, needles with yellow bands, trunks with patterned or mother-of-pearl-like bark and varied forms.

Growing

Pines grow best in **full sun**. These trees adapt to most **well-drained** soils but do not tolerate polluted urban conditions.

Tips

Pines can be used as specimen trees, as hedges or to create windbreaks. Smaller cultivars can be included in shrub or mixed borders. These trees are not heavy feeders; fertilizing will encourage rapid new growth that is weak and susceptible to pests and disease.

Recommended

There are many available pines, both in tree and shrubby dwarf varieties. Check with your local garden center or nursery to find out what is available.

The Austrian pine, P. nigra, *was often recommended as the most urban-tolerant pine, but overplanting has led to severe disease problems, some of which can kill a tree in a single growing season.*

Features: upright, columnar or spreading, evergreen tree; foliage; bark; cones; habit
Height: 2–120' **Spread:** 2–60'
Hardiness: zones 2–8

Potentilla
Potentilla

P. fruticosa (above & below)

Potentilla is a fuss-free shrub that blooms madly all summer. The cheery, yellow-flowered variety is often seen, but cultivars with flowers in shades of pink, red and tangerine have broadened the use of this reliable shrub.

Growing
Potentilla prefers **full sun** but tolerates partial or light shade. The soil should be of **poor to average fertility** and **well drained**. This plant tolerates most conditions, including sandy or clay soil and wet or dry conditions. Established plants are drought tolerant. Too much fertilizer or too rich a soil will encourage weak, floppy, disease-prone growth.

Tips
Potentilla is useful in a shrub or mixed border. Smaller cultivars can be included in rock gardens and on rock walls. On slopes that are steep or awkward to mow, potentilla can prevent soil erosion and reduce the time spent maintaining the lawn. Potentilla can also be used to form a low, informal hedge.

If your potentilla's flowers fade in the bright sun or in hot weather, try moving the plant to a more sheltered location. Colors should revive in fall as the weather cools. Yellow-flowered plants are the least likely to be affected by heat and sun.

Recommended
Of the many cultivars of *P. fruticosa*, the following are a few of the most popular and interesting. **'Abbotswood'** is one of the best white-flowered cultivars; **'Pink Beauty'** bears pink, semi-double flowers; **'Tangerine'** has orange flowers; and **'Yellow Gem'** has bright yellow flowers.

Also called: shrubby cinquefoil
Features: mounding, deciduous shrub; flowers; foliage; habit **Height:** 12"–5'
Spread: 12"–5' **Hardiness:** zones 2–8

Redbud

Cercis

Redbud is an outstanding spring treasure. Deep magenta flowers bloom before the leaves emerge, and their impact is intense. As the buds open, the flowers turn pink, covering the long, thin branches in pastel clouds.

Growing

Redbud grows well in **full sun, partial shade** or **light shade**. The soil should be a **fertile, deep loam** that is **moist** and **well drained**. This plant has tender roots and does not like being transplanted.

Tips

Redbud can be used as a specimen tree, in a shrub or mixed border or in a woodland garden.

Recommended

C. canadensis (eastern redbud) is a spreading, multi-stemmed tree that bears red, purple or pink flowers. The young foliage is bronze, fading to green over summer and turning bright yellow in fall. Many beautiful cultivars are available.

C. canadensis (above & below)

Redbud is not as long-lived as many other trees, so use its delicate beauty to supplement more permanent trees.

Features: rounded or spreading, multi-stemmed, deciduous tree or shrub; spring flowers; fall foliage **Height:** 20–30' **Spread:** 25–35'
Hardiness: zones 4–9

Rhododendron
Rhododendron

R. Northern Lights Hybrids (above), azalea hybrid (below)

Even when not covered in a stunning display of brightly colored flowers, rhododendrons are wonderful landscape plants.

Growing

Rhododendrons and evergreen azaleas grow best in **partial shade** or **light shade**, whereas the deciduous azaleas typically grow best in **full sun** or **partial shade**. Choose a location that is protected from drying winter winds and avoid hot, sun-scorched locations. The soil should be **fertile, humus rich, acidic, moist** and

well drained. A good mulch is important to keep the soil moist and protect the shallow roots of these plants.

Tips

Rhododendrons and azaleas perform best and look good when planted in groups. Use them in shrub or mixed borders, in woodland gardens and in sheltered rock gardens.

Recommended

These bushy shrubs vary greatly in size and hardiness, may be evergreen or deciduous and bear flowers in a huge range of colors. There are hundreds of rhododendron and azalea species, hybrids and cultivars available. Visit your local garden center or specialty grower to see what is available.

Also called: azalea **Features:** upright, mounding, rounded, evergreen or deciduous shrub; late-winter to early-summer flowers; foliage; habit **Height:** 2–12' **Spread:** 24"–12' **Hardiness:** zones 3–8

Scotch Heather
Calluna

C. *vulgaris* cultivar (above & below)

Scotch heather is beautiful when mass planted or used individually in a mixed border.

Growing
Scotch heather grows best in **full sun**. The soil should be of **poor to average fertility, acidic, moist** and **well drained**. Ample snow cover will protect Scotch heather during cold winters. Mulch if snow cover is inconsistent. Avoid damaging the shallow roots when working the soil near these plants.

Tips
Scotch heather makes a dense, weed-smothering groundcover. It is tolerant of coastal conditions and is useful for binding sandy soils. It makes an attractive edging plant for beds and borders and in rock gardens.

Also called: heather, ling, Scots heather
Features: mat-forming shrub; evergreen foliage; summer to fall flowers
Height: 4–30" **Spread:** 24–30"
Hardiness: zones 3–7

Recommended
C. vulgaris is a mat-forming, evergreen shrub with densely branched, erect stems. It bears pink flowers from mid-summer to fall. The scale-like, gray-green foliage becomes purple tinged in winter. There are hundreds of cultivars, but many of them are only available in Europe. Cultivars include plants with red, pink, white or purple flowers; dark green, yellow, orange-yellow, bronze and variegated green-white foliage; and bronze, red, red-orange or purple winter colors.

Serviceberry
Amelanchier

A. canadensis (above)

Serviceberry fruit can be used in place of blueberries in any recipe, having a similar but generally sweeter flavor.

The *Amelanchier* species are first-rate North American natives, bearing lacy, white flowers in spring, followed by edible berries. In fall, the foliage color ranges from a glowing apricot to deep red.

Growing
Serviceberries grow well in **full sun** or **light shade**. They prefer **acidic** soil that is **fertile, humus rich, moist** and **well drained**. Established plants adapt to periodic droughts.

Tips
With spring flowers, edible fruit, attractive leaves that turn red in fall and often-artistic branch growth, serviceberries make beautiful specimen plants or even shade trees in small gardens. The shrubbier forms can be grown along the edges of a woodland or in a border. In the wild these trees are often found growing near water sources and are beautiful beside ponds or streams.

Recommended
Several species and hybrids are available. A few popular serviceberries are *A. arborea* (downy serviceberry, Juneberry), a small single- or multi-stemmed tree; *A. canadensis* (shadblow serviceberry), a large, upright, suckering shrub; and *A.* x *grandiflora* (apple serviceberry), a small, spreading, often multi-stemmed tree. All three have white flowers, purple fruit and good fall color.

Also called: saskatoon, juneberry
Features: single- or multi-stemmed, deciduous, large shrub or small tree; spring or early-summer flowers; edible fruit; fall color; habit; bark **Height:** 4–30'
Spread: 4–30' **Hardiness:** zones 3–9

Seven-Son Flower

Heptacodium

As a smallish tree with fragrant, white flowers in September followed by red sepals (the outer ring of flower parts) and fruit, seven-son flower makes a welcome addition to our plant palette.

H. miconioides (above & below)

This plant is a fairly recent introduction to North American gardens and may not be available in all garden centers.

Growing

Seven-son flower prefers **full sun** but tolerates partial shade. The soil should be of **average fertility, moist** and **well drained**, though this plant is fairly tolerant of most soil conditions, including dry and acidic soil.

Tips

This large shrub can be used in place of a shade tree on a small property. Planted near a patio or deck, the plant will provide light shade, and its fragrant flowers can be enjoyed in late summer. In a border it provides light shade to plants growing below it, and the dark green leaves make a good backdrop for bright perennial and annual flowers.

Seven-son flower's tolerance of dry and salty soils makes it useful where salty snow may be shoveled off walkways in winter and where watering may be minimal in summer.

Recommended

H. miconioides is a large, multi-stemmed shrub or small tree with peeling, tan bark and dark green leaves that may become tinged with purple in fall. Clusters of fragrant, creamy white flowers have persistent sepals that turn dark pink to bright red in mid- to late fall and surround small, purple-red fruit.

Features: upright to spreading, multi-stemmed, deciduous shrub or small tree; habit; bark; fall flowers **Height:** 15–20' **Spread:** 8–15' **Hardiness:** zones 5–8

Smokebush

Cotinus

C. coggygria 'Royal Purple' (above), C. coggygria (below)

Bright fall color, adaptability, variable sizes and forms, and flowers of differing colors make smokebush and all its cultivars excellent additions to the garden.

Growing

Smokebush grows well in **full sun** or **partial shade**. It prefers soil of **average fertility** that is **moist** and **well drained**, but it adapts to all but very wet soils.

Tips

Smokebush can be used in a shrub or mixed border, as a single specimen or in groups. It is a good choice for a rocky hillside planting.

Recommended

C. coggygria is a bushy, rounded shrub that develops large, puffy plumes of flowers that start out green and gradually turn a pinky gray. The green foliage turns red, orange and yellow in fall. Many cultivars are available, including purple-leaved varieties.

Try encouraging a clematis vine to wind its way through the spreading branches of a smokebush.

Also called: smoketree
Features: bushy, rounded, spreading, deciduous tree or shrub; early-summer flowers; summer and fall foliage
Height: 10–15' **Spread:** 10–15'
Hardiness: zones 4–8

Snowbell

Styrax

S. *obassia* (above & right)

Snowbells are easy to admire for their delicate, shapely appearance and the dangling flowers clustered along the undersides of their branches.

Growing

Snowbells grow well in **full sun, partial shade** or **light shade**. The soil should be **fertile, humus rich, neutral to acidic, moist** and **well drained**.

Tips

Snowbells can be used to provide light shade in shrub or mixed borders. They can also be included in woodland gardens, and they make interesting specimens near entryways or patios.

Features: upright, rounded, spreading or columnar, deciduous tree; late-spring to early-summer flowers; foliage; habit
Height: 20–40' **Spread:** 20–30'
Hardiness: zones 4–8

Recommended

S. ***obassia*** (fragrant snowbell) is a broad, columnar tree that bears white flowers in long clusters at the branch ends in early summer.

Another commonly available species is S. *japonica* (Japanese snowbell); it is no longer recommended because it is becoming invasive in native forests.

Plant a snowbell next to your patio so you can admire the flowers from below as you stretch out in a lounge chair.

Spirea
Spiraea

S. japonica 'Goldmound' (above), *S. x vanhouttei* (below)

Spireas, seen in so many gardens and with dozens of cultivars, remain undeniable favorites. With a wide range of forms, sizes and colors of both foliage and flowers, spireas have many possible uses in the landscape.

Growing
Spireas prefer **full sun**, but to help prevent foliage burn, provide protection from very hot afternoon sun. The soil should be **fertile, acidic, moist** and **well drained**.

Spireas are very popular ornamental shrubs because they adapt to many situations and require only minimal care once established.

Tips
Spireas are used in shrub or mixed borders, in rock gardens and as informal screens and hedges.

Recommended
Many species and cultivars of spirea are available. Two popular hybrid groups are listed below. **S. x bumalda** (*S. japonica* 'Bumalda') is a low, broad, mounded shrub with pink flowers. It is rarely grown in favor of the many cultivars, which also have pink flowers, but often have brightly colored foliage. **S. x vanhouttei** (bridal wreath spirea, Vanhoutte spirea) is a dense, bushy shrub with arching branches that bears clusters of white flowers. Check with your local nursery or garden center to see what cultivars are available.

Features: round, bushy, deciduous shrub; summer flowers; habit **Height:** 1–10' **Spread:** 1–12' **Hardiness:** zones 3–9

Spruce

Picea

The spruce is one of the most commonly grown and commonly abused evergreens. Grow spruces where they have enough room to spread, then let them branch all the way to the ground.

Growing

Spruce trees grow best in **full sun**. The soil should be **deep, moist, well drained** and **neutral to acidic**. These trees generally don't like hot, dry or polluted conditions. Spruces are best grown from small, young stock as they dislike being transplanted when larger or more mature.

Tips

Spruces are used as specimen trees. The dwarf and slow-growing cultivars can also be used in shrub or mixed borders. These trees look most attractive when allowed to keep their lower branches.

Recommended

Spruces are generally upright pyramidal trees, but cultivars may have low-growing, wide-spreading or even weeping habits. ***P. abies*** (Norway spruce), ***P. glauca*** (white spruce), ***P. omorika*** (Serbian spruce), ***P. pungens*** (Colorado spruce) and their cultivars are popular and commonly available.

P. glauca 'Conica' (above), *P. pungens* var. *glauca* 'Moerheim' (below)

Oil-based pesticides such as dormant oil can take the blue out of your blue-needled spruces. Growth that fills in after this will have the blue color.

Features: conical or columnar, evergreen tree or shrub; foliage; cones; habit
Height: 2–80' **Spread:** 2–25'
Hardiness: zones 2–8

Summersweet Clethra
Clethra

C. alnifolia 'September Beauty' (above)
C. alnifolia 'Paniculata' (below)

Summersweet clethra is one of the best shrubs for adding fragrance to your garden and attracting butterflies and other pollinators.

Growing

Summersweet clethra grows best in **light or partial shade**. The soil should be **fertile, humus rich, acidic, moist** and **well drained**.

Tips

Although not aggressive, this shrub tends to sucker, forming a colony of stems. Use it in a border or in a woodland garden. The light shade along the edge of a woodland is also an ideal location.

Recommended

C. alnifolia is a large, rounded, upright, colony-forming shrub. It grows 3–8' tall, spreads 3–6' and bears attractive spikes of white flowers in mid- to late summer. The foliage turns yellow in fall. Several cultivars are available, including pink-flowered selections.

Summersweet clethra is useful in damp, shaded gardens, where the late-season flowers are much appreciated.

Also called: sweet pepperbush, sweetspire **Features:** rounded, suckering deciduous shrub; fragrant, summer flowers; attractive habit; colorful fall foliage
Height: 2–8' **Spread:** 3–8'
Hardiness: zones 3–9

Viburnum
Viburnum

Good fall color, attractive form, shade tolerance, scented flowers and attractive fruit put the viburnums in a class by themselves.

Growing

Viburnums grow well in **full sun, partial shade** or **light shade**. The soil should be of **average fertility, moist** and **well drained**. Viburnums tolerate both alkaline and acidic soils.

These plants will look neatest if deadheaded, but this practice will prevent fruits from forming. Fruiting is better when more than one plant of a species is grown.

Tips

Viburnums can be used in borders and woodland gardens. They are a good choice for plantings near swimming pools.

V. opulus (above), *V. plicatum* var. *tomentosum* (below)

Recommended

Many viburnum species, hybrids and cultivars are available. A few popular ones include **V. carlesii** (Korean spice viburnum), a dense, bushy, rounded, deciduous shrub with white or pink, spice-scented flowers (Zones 5–8); **V. opulus** (European cranberrybush, Guelder-rose), a rounded, spreading, deciduous shrub with lacy-looking flower clusters (Zones 3–8); **V. plicatum** var. **tomentosum** (doublefile viburnum), with a graceful, horizontal branching pattern that gives the shrub a layered effect and lacy-looking white flower clusters (Zones 5–8); and **V. trilobum** (American cranberrybush, highbush cranberry), a dense, rounded shrub with clusters of white flowers followed by edible red fruit (Zones 2–7).

Features: bushy or spreading, evergreen, semi-evergreen or deciduous shrub; flowers (some fragrant); summer and fall foliage; fruit; habit **Height:** 18"–20' **Spread:** 18"–15' **Hardiness:** zones 2–8

Weigela
Weigela

W. florida MIDNIGHT WINE ('Elvera'; above), *W. florida* (below)

Weigelas have been improved through breeding, and specimens with more compact forms, longer flowering periods and greater cold tolerance are now available.

Growing
Weigelas prefer **full sun** but tolerate partial shade. The soil should be **fertile** and **well drained**. These plants adapt to most well-drained soil conditions.

Tips
Weigelas can be used in shrub or mixed borders, in open woodland gardens and as informal barrier plantings.

Recommended
W. florida is a spreading shrub with arching branches that bear clusters of dark pink flowers. Many hybrids and cultivars are available, including dwarf varieties, those with red-, pink- or white-flowers and others with purple, bronze or yellow foliage.

Weigela is one of the longest-blooming shrubs, with the main flush of blooms lasting as long as six weeks. It often re-blooms if sheared lightly after the first flowers fade.

Features: upright or low, spreading, deciduous shrub; late-spring to early-summer flowers; foliage; habit **Height:** 1–9' **Spread:** 1–12' **Hardiness:** zones 3–8

Willow

Salix

S. *integra* 'Hakuro Nishiki' (above)

These fast-growing deciduous shrubs or trees can have colorful or twisted stems or foliage and come in a huge range of growth habits and sizes.

Growing

Willows grow best in **full sun**. The soil should be of **average fertility, moist** and **well drained**. Some of the shrubby species are drought resistant.

Tips

Large tree willows should be reserved for large spaces and are attractive near water features. Smaller willows can be used as small specimen trees or in shrub and mixed borders. Small, trailing forms can be included in rock gardens and along retaining walls.

Recommended

S. alba 'Tristis' is a deciduous, rounded tree with delicate, flexible, weeping branches. The young growth and fall leaves are bright yellow (zones 4–8). *S.* x *grahamii* (Graham's willow) is a shrubby, dwarf hybrid. A low, trailing cultivar is available. *S. integra* 'Hakuro Nishiki' (dappled willow, Japanese dappled willow) is a spreading shrub with supple, arching branches that appear almost weeping. The young shoots are orange-pink and the leaves are dappled green, cream and pink (Zones 5–8). *S.* SCARLET CURLS (*S.* 'Sarcuzam') is an upright, shrubby tree with curled and twisted branches and leaves. The young stems are reddish and become redder after a frost, creating an attractive winter display (Zones 5–8).

Features: bushy or arching shrub or spreading or weeping tree; summer and fall foliage; stems; habit **Height:** 1–65' **Spread:** 3–65' **Hardiness:** zones 3–8

Witchhazel
Hamamelis

H. x intermedia (above)

Witchhazel is an investment in happiness. It blooms in early spring, the flowers last for weeks and their spicy fragrance awakens the senses. Then in fall, the handsome leaves develop overlapping bands of orange, yellow and red.

Growing
Witchhazels grow best in a **sheltered** spot with **full sun** or **light shade**. The soil should be of **average fertility, neutral to acidic, moist** and **well drained**.

Tips
Witchhazels work well individually or in groups. They can be used as specimen plants, in shrub or mixed borders or in woodland gardens. As small trees, they are ideal for space-limited gardens.

The unique flowers have long, narrow, crinkled petals that give the plant a spidery appearance when in bloom. If the weather gets too cold, the petals will roll up, protecting the flowers and extending the flowering season.

Recommended
H. x *intermedia* is a vase-shaped, spreading shrub that bears fragrant clusters of yellow, orange or red flowers. The leaves turn attractive shades of orange, red and bronze in fall. Cultivars with flowers in shades of red, yellow or orange are available.

Features: spreading, deciduous shrub or small tree; fragrant, early-spring flowers; summer and fall foliage; habit **Height:** 6–20' **Spread:** 6–20' **Hardiness:** zones 5–9

Yew
Taxus

$\mathcal{F}$rom sweeping hedges to commanding speci-mens, yews can serve many purposes in the garden. They are the only reliable evergreens for deep shade.

Growing

Yews grow well in any light conditions from **full sun to full shade**. The soil should be **fertile, moist** and **well drained**. These trees tolerate windy, dry and polluted con-ditions and soils of any acidity. They dislike excessive heat, however, and on the hotter south or southwest side of a building they may suffer nee-dle scorch.

Tips

Yews can be used in borders or as specimens, hedges, topiary and groundcover.

T. x *media* 'Sunburst' (above)

Male and female flowers are borne on separate plants. Both must be present for the attractive red arils (seed cups) to form.

Recommended

T. **x** *media* (English Japanese yew), a cross between *T. baccata* (English yew) and *T. cuspidata* (Japanese yew), has the vigor of the English yew and the cold hardiness of the Japanese yew. It forms a rounded, upright tree or shrub, though the size and form can vary among the many cultivars.

Features: evergreen; conical or columnar tree or bushy or spreading shrub; foliage; habit; red seed cups **Height:** 1–70'
Spread: 1–30' **Hardiness:** zones 4–7

Altissimo

Climbing Floribunda Rose

Italian for 'in the highest,' Altissimo is an apt name for this high-climbing, high-quality, highly disease-resistant rose.

Growing

Altissimo grows best in **full sun** in a **warm, sheltered** location. The soil should be **fertile, slightly acidic, humus rich, moist** and **well drained**. The canes must be attached to a sturdy support.

Tips

Altissimo's stiff, sturdy stems form a bushy, spreading plant that can be grown as a large shrub or trained to climb a wall, trellis, porch or pergola.

When cut, the long-stemmed blooms are long lasting and unfading. They can be used in a variety of arrangements.

Recommended

Rosa '**Altissimo**' has large, matte, serrated, leathery, dark green foliage and single flowers borne in clusters for most of the growing season on both new and old growth. In a warm location it can grow to cover a wall.

George Delbard of Delbard-Chabert developed Altissimo in 1966 in France. It was a seedling of Tenor, a red climber created by Delbard.

Also called: altus, sublimely single
Features: vigorous climber; slightly clove-scented, blood red early-summer to fall flowers **Height:** 8–9' **Spread:** 5–8'
Hardiness: zones 5–9

Apothecary's Rose

Species Rose

This rose has been cultivated since the 13th century and was used in herbal medicine to treat inflammation, aches, pains and insomnia.

Growing

Apothecary's Rose prefers **full sun** but tolerates afternoon shade. The soil should be **average to fertile, slightly acidic, humus rich, moist** and **well drained**. The suckers it produces should be removed once flowering is complete.

Tips

Apothecary's Rose can be grown as a specimen, in a shrub border or as a hedge. It can be naturalized or used to prevent soil erosion on a bank too steep for mowing. The flowers are very fragrant; plant this shrub near windows, doors and frequently used pathways.

Recommended

Rosa gallica **'Officinalis'** is a bushy, rounded, vigorous, disease-resistant shrub with bristly stems and dark green leaves. One flush of semi-double flowers is produced each year in late spring or early summer. *Rosa gallica* **'Versicolor'** has white or light pink flowers with darker pink splashes and stripes.

This rose is known for its culinary and medicinal value and its use in crafts, particularly in potpourri.

Also called: red damask, red rose of Lancaster
Features: rounded habit; fresh and intensely fragrant, white, crimson purple, pinkish red early-summer flowers; dark red hips
Height: 30–48" **Spread:** 30–48"
Hardiness: zones 4–10

Aspen
Groundcover Rose

The dense growth of Aspen completely obscures the ground beneath its low, sprawling branches.

Growing
Aspen grows best in **full sun**. The soil should be **average to fertile, humus rich, slightly acidic, moist** and **well drained**.

Tips
Although not a true groundcover, Aspen is useful for filling in large areas. It can also be used as a low hedge or in a mixed border where it may require some pruning to reduce its spread. Its spreading habit makes it ideal for hanging baskets and urn-style planters where the branches, with their bright yellow flowers, cascade over the edges.

Recommended
Rosa 'Aspen' is a bushy, low-growing, spreading plant with light green foliage. It produces semi-double flowers over a long period in summer.

Unlike many yellow roses, Aspen is highly resistant to blackspot and is very winter hardy.

Features: mounding, spreading habit; intensely fragrant, yellow summer to fall flowers **Height:** 14–16" **Spread:** 24–36" **Hardiness:** zones 4–9

Belle Amour

Old Garden Rose

Classified as an ancient damask rose, Belle Amour is extremely easy to grow, even in the worst soil or environmental conditions.

Growing
Belle Amour grows best in **full sun**. The soil should be **average to fertile, humus rich, slightly acidic, moist** and **well drained**, but this rose tolerates most soil conditions once established.

Tips
Old garden roses like Belle Amour seem most at home in an English country-style garden, but they can also be used in borders and as specimens.

Recommended
Rosa **'Belle Amour'** is an upright shrub with gray-green foliage. It bears fully double, camellia-like blooms in a single flush in late spring or early summer. The bright red hips persist into winter.

Old garden roses are those that were discovered or hybridized before 1867, and they are admired for their delicate beauty, old-fashioned appearance and fantastic fragrance. They are the ancestors of many roses found today.

Some claim that Belle Amour is a cross between an alba and a damask rose.

Features: upright habit; spicy, myrrh-scented, light to medium pink early-summer flowers; red hips **Height:** 5–6' **Spread:** 3–4'
Hardiness: zones 3–10

Cupcake
Miniature Rose

Cupcake has strong, healthy growth, and blooms throughout the season.

Growing

Cupcake grows best in **full sun**. The soil should be **fertile, humus rich, slightly acidic, moist** and **well drained**. Deadhead to keep plants neat and to encourage continuous blooming.

Tips

Miniature roses like Cupcake are sometimes used as annual bedding plants. As annual or perennial shrubs, they can be included in window boxes, planters and mixed containers. In a bed or border they can be grouped together or planted individually to accentuate specific areas. They also can be used as groundcover or to create a low hedge.

Recommended

Rosa 'Cupcake' is a compact, bushy shrub with glossy green foliage that resembles a miniature version of a high-centered, large-flowered modern rose. It produces small clusters of double flowers all summer.

Cupcake, a disease-resistant miniature rose, requires very little maintenance. It can be brought indoors for the winter and enjoyed as a houseplant until spring. It will do best in a cool, well-ventilated room.

Features: bushy habit; slightly fragrant, light to medium pink early-summer to fall flowers
Height: 12–18" **Spread:** 12–14"
Hardiness: zones 5–11

Distant Drums

Modern Shrub Rose

Distant Drums bears uniquely colored flowers; the medium to dark mauve buds open to pale mauve with peachy, tan-centered blossoms.

Growing

Distant Drums grows best in **full sun** in a **warm, sheltered** location. The soil should be **fertile, humus rich, slightly acidic, moist** and **well drained**. This rose is reliably resistant to blackspot and powdery mildew.

Tips

Distant Drums makes a lovely addition to mixed beds and borders and has an attractive- enough form to be used as a specimen plant. Plant it near a window or along a well-used pathway where the fragrance can be enjoyed.

Recommended

Rosa **'Distant Drums'** is an upright, bushy rose with dark green, leathery foliage. Flowers are produced singly or in clusters of up to 10 blooms from mid-summer through to fall.

Dr. Griffith Buck developed this rose and introduced it into commerce in 1985 as another striking addition to his collection.

Features: bushy habit; intensely fragrant, double, peachy tan summer to fall flowers with mauve edges **Height:** 3–4' **Spread:** 3–4'
Hardiness: zones 4–9

Golden Celebration

English (Austin) Shrub Rose

David Austin roses are famous for their scent, and Golden Celebration is no exception. The fruity smell of these flowers is strong enough to catch the attention of any passerby.

Growing
Golden Celebration grows best in **full sun** in a **warm, sheltered** location. The soil should be **fertile, humus rich, slightly acidic, moist** and **well drained**. Deadhead to keep plants tidy and to encourage continuous blooming. Protection may be required to overwinter this rose successfully.

Tips
Austin roses such as Golden Celebration have many uses and are often included in borders or used as specimens. With training, Golden Celebration can also be grown as a climber. Plant it near a window, door or pathway where its fragrance can best be enjoyed.

Recommended
Rosa '**Golden Celebration**' forms a rounded shrub with dark green, glossy foliage and flexible canes that sway or bend under the weight of the double flowers. It is one of many Austin roses that are also available in shades of pink, orange, apricot, yellow or white.

Golden Celebration is considered one of the largest-flowered and most stunning Austin roses ever developed.

Features: attractive, rounded habit; fruit scented, golden yellow early-summer to fall flowers **Height:** 4–5' **Spread:** 4–5'
Hardiness: zones 5–9

Hansa

Rugosa Shrub Rose

Hansa, first introduced in 1905, is one of the most durable, long-lived and versatile roses.

Growing

Hansa grows best in **full sun**. The soil should preferably be **average to fertile, humus rich, slightly acidic, moist** and **well drained**, but this durable rose adapts to most soils, from sandy to silty clay. Remove a few of the oldest canes every few years to keep plants blooming vigorously.

Tips

Rugosa roses like Hansa make good additions to mixed borders and beds, and they can also be used as hedges or specimens. They are often used on steep banks to prevent soil erosion. Their prickly branches deter people from walking across flower beds and compacting the soil. Tolerant of coastal conditions, they are often included in seashore plantings and gardens.

Recommended

Rosa 'Hansa' is a bushy shrub with arching canes and leathery, deeply veined, bright green leaves. The double flowers are produced all summer. The bright orange hips persist into winter. Other rugosa roses include '**Blanc Double de Coubert**,' which produces white, double flowers all summer.

Rosa rugosa is a wide-spreading plant with disease-resistant foliage, a trait it has passed on to many hybrids and cultivars.

Features: dense, arching habit; clove-scented, mauve purple or mauve red early-summer to fall flowers; orange-red hips **Height:** 4–5' **Spread:** 5–6' **Hardiness:** zones 3–9

Iceberg
Floribunda Rose

Over 40 years have passed since this exceptional rose was first introduced, and its dainty, continuous blooms are still popular today.

Growing

Iceberg grows best in **full sun**. The soil should be **fertile, humus rich, slightly acidic, moist** and **well drained**.

Iceberg blooms tend to be flushed with pink when the nights are cool. Rain or dewdrops on the petals can also stain the petals pink.

Tips

Iceberg is a popular addition to mixed borders and beds, and also works well as a specimen. Plant it in a well-used area or near a window where the fragrance of its flowers can best be enjoyed. This rose can also be included in large planters or patio containers.

Recommended

Rosa 'Iceberg' is a vigorous shrub with a rounded, bushy habit and light green foliage. The clusters of semi-double flowers are produced in several flushes from early to mid-summer. A climbing variation of this rose is also available.

Also called: fée des neiges
Features: bushy habit; strong, sweet fragrance; white, early to mid-summer flowers, sometimes flushed with pink during cool or wet weather **Height:** 3–4'
Spread: 36–48" **Hardiness:** zones 5–9

Knockout

Modern Shrub Rose

This rose is simply one of the best new shrub roses to hit the market in years. It graces the garden with a good rose fragrance combined with exceptional disease resistance.

Growing

Knockout grows best in **full sun**. The soil should be **fertile, humus rich, slightly acidic, moist** and **well drained**. Blooming is most prolific in warm weather, but the flowers are a deeper red in cooler weather. Deadhead lightly to keep the plant tidy and to encourage prolific blooming.

Tips

This vigorous, attractive rose makes a good addition to a mixed bed or border. Equally attractive as a specimen or in groups, it can be mass planted to create a large display.

Recommended

Rosa 'Knockout' has a lovely rounded form with glossy green leaves that turn to shades of burgundy in fall. The bright cherry red flowers are borne in clusters of 3–15 almost all summer and in early fall. The orange-red hips last into winter. A light pink selection called **'Blushing Knockout'** as well as **'Double Knockout'** and **'Pink Knockout'** are available. All have excellent disease resistance.

If you've been afraid that roses need too much care, you'll appreciate the hardiness and disease resistance of this low-maintenance beauty.

Also called: Knock Out
Features: rounded habit; cherry red flowers with a light tea-rose scent from mid-summer to fall; disease resistant **Height:** 3–4'
Spread: 3–4' **Hardiness:** zones 4–10

Rosa glauca
Species Rose

This species rose is a gardener's dream; it's hardy and has good disease resistance, with striking foliage in summer and colorful hips in winter.

Growing
Rosa glauca grows best and develops contrasting foliage color in **full sun** but tolerates some shade. The soil should be **average to fertile, humus rich, slightly acidic, moist** and **well drained**, but this rose adapts to most soils, from sandy soil to silty clay.

Cut a few of the oldest canes to the ground every few years to encourage younger, more colorful stems to grow in. Removing spent flowers won't prolong the blooming period, and the more flowers you leave the more hips will form.

Tips
With its unusual foliage color, *Rosa glauca* makes a good addition to mixed borders and beds, and it can also be used as a hedge or specimen.

Recommended
Rosa glauca (*R. rubrifolia*) is a bushy shrub with arching, purple-tinged canes and delicate, purple-tinged, blue-green leaves. The single, star-like flowers bloom in clusters in late spring. The dark red hips persist until spring.

Rosa glauca is extremely popular with rosarians and novice gardeners alike because of its hardiness, disease resistance, dainty blooms and foliage color. It received the Royal Horticultural Society Award of Garden Merit, proof of its dependable performance.

Also called: red-leaved rose
Features: dense, arching, habit; purple- or red-tinged foliage; white-centered, mauve pink late-spring flowers; persistent, dark red hips **Height:** 6–10' **Spread:** 5–6'
Hardiness: zones 2–9

Black-Eyed Susan Vine
Thunbergia

Black-eyed Susan vine is a useful, annual-flowering vine whose simple flowers dot the plant, giving it a cheerful, welcoming appearance.

Growing
Black-eyed Susan vines do well in **full sun**, **partial shade** or **light shade**. Grow it in **fertile, moist, well-drained** soil that is high in **organic matter**.

Tips
Black-eyed Susan vines can be trained to twine up and around fences, walls, trees and shrubs. They are also attractive trailing down from the top of a rock garden or rock wall or growing in mixed containers and hanging baskets.

Recommended
T. alata is a vigorous, twining climber. It bears yellow flowers, often with dark centers, in summer and fall. Cultivars with large flowers in yellow, orange or white are available.

T. grandiflora (skyflower vine, blue trumpet vine) is less commonly available than *T. alata*. It tends to bloom late, in early to mid-fall. This twining climber bears stunning, pale violet-blue flowers. **'Alba'** has white flowers.

T. alata 'Red Shades' (above), *T. alata* (below)

Plants grown in containers and hanging baskets can be brought indoors for winter if acclimated to the lower light levels and kept in a bright, cool location.

Features: twining habit; yellow, orange, violet-blue, creamy white, dark-centered flowers **Height:** 5' or more **Spread:** 5' or more **Hardiness:** tender perennial treated as an annual

Boston Ivy
Parthenocissus

P. tricuspidata 'Fenway Park'

P. tricuspidata 'Lowii'

Boston ivy is a handsome vine that establishes quickly and, with patience, provides an air of age and permanence, even on new structures.

Growing

These vines grow well in any light from **full sun to full shade**. The soil should be **fertile** and **well drained**. The plants adapt to clay or sandy soils.

Boston ivy can cover the sides of buildings and help keep them cool in the summer heat. Cut plants back as needed to keep windows and doors accessible.

Tips

Boston ivy can cover an entire building, given enough time. They do not require support because they have clinging rootlets that can adhere to just about any surface, even smooth wood, vinyl or metal. Give the plants a lot of space and let them cover a wall, fence or arbor.

Recommended

P. tricuspidata (Boston ivy, Japanese creeper) has dark green, three-lobed leaves that turn red in fall.

Features: summer and fall foliage; clinging habit **Height:** 30–70' **Spread:** 30–70' **Hardiness:** zones 4–8

Clematis

Clematis

Clematis is the queen of vines; there are so many species, hybrids and cultivars that it is possible to have one in bloom all season.

Growing

Clematis plants prefer **full sun** but tolerate partial shade. The soil should be **fertile, humus rich, moist** and **well drained**. These vines enjoy warm, sunny weather, but the roots prefer to be cool. A thick layer of mulch or a planting of low, shade-providing perennials will protect the tender roots. Clematis are quite cold hardy but fare best when protected from winter wind. The rootball of vining clematis should be planted about 2" beneath the surface of the soil.

Tips

Clematis vines can climb up structures such as trellises, railings, fences and arbors. They can also be allowed to grow over shrubs and up trees and can be used as groundcover.

Recommended

There are many species, hybrids and cultivars of clematis. The flower forms, blooming times and sizes of the plants can vary. There are also low-growing shrub and perennial selections. Check with your local garden center to see what is available.

C. 'Jackmanii Rubra' (above)
C. 'Gravetye Beauty' (below)

Features: twining habit; blue, purple, pink, yellow, red, white, early to late-summer flowers; decorative seedheads **Height:** 10–17' or more **Spread:** 5' or more **Hardiness:** zones 3–8

Climbing Hydrangea
Hydrangea

H. anomala subsp. *petiolaris* (above & below)

A mature climbing hydrangea can cover an entire wall, and with its dark, glossy leaves and delicate, lacy flowers, it is quite possibly one of the most stunning climbing plants available.

Growing

Hydrangeas prefer **partial or light shade** but tolerate full sun or full shade. The soil should be of **average to high fertility,**

Climbing hydrangea produces the most flowers when it is exposed to some direct sunlight each day. Have patience, as this vine may need to establish for a couple of years before it begins blooming.

humus rich, moist and **well drained**. These plants perform best in cool, moist conditions, so be sure to mulch their roots.

Tips

Climbing hydrangea climbs up trees, walls, fences, pergolas and arbors. It clings by means of aerial roots, so needs no narrow supports to twine around, just a somewhat textured surface. It also grows over rocks, can be used as a groundcover and can be trained to form a small tree or shrub.

Recommended

H. anomala* subsp. *petiolaris (*H. petiolaris*) is a clinging vine with dark, glossy green leaves that sometimes turn an attractive yellow in fall. For more than a month in mid-summer, the vine is covered with white, lacy-looking flowers, and the entire plant appears to be veiled in a lacy mist.

Features: white flowers; clinging habit; exfoliating bark **Height:** 50–80'
Spread: 50–80' **Hardiness:** zones 4–9

Cup-and-Saucer Vine

Cobaea

C. scandens (above & below)

Cup-and-saucer vine is a vigorous annual climber native to Mexico that produces frilly, purple flowers from spring until frost.

Growing

Cup-and-saucer vine prefers **full sun**. The soil should be **well drained** and of **average fertility**. This plant is fond of hot weather and does best if planted in a sheltered site with a southern exposure. Set the seeds on edge when planting them, and barely cover them with soil.

Tips

Grow this vine up a trellis, over an arbor or along a chain-link fence. Cup-and-saucer vine requires a sturdy support in order to climb. It uses grabbing hooks so won't be able to grow up a wall without something to hold on to. It can be trained to fill almost any space. In hanging baskets, the vines will climb the hanger and spill over the edges.

Recommended

C. scandens is a vigorous climbing vine with flowers that are creamy green when they open and mature to deep purple. **Var. *alba*** has white flowers.

These tender plants can be cut back a bit in fall and overwintered indoors. Plants grown in hanging baskets are the easiest to move indoors.

Also called: cathedral bells
Features: purple or white flowers; clinging habit; long blooming period **Height:** 15–25'
Spread: 15–25' **Hardiness:** tender perennial treated as an annual

Hardy Kiwi
Actinidia

A. arguta 'Ananasaya' (above), *A. arguta* (below)

Hardy kiwi is handsome in its simplicity, and its lush green leaves, vigor and adaptability make it very useful, especially on difficult sites.

Growing

Hardy kiwi vines grow best in **full sun**. The soil should be **fertile** and **well drained**. These plants require shelter from strong winds.

Tips

These vines need a sturdy structure to twine around. Pergolas, arbors and sufficiently large and sturdy fences provide good support. Given a trellis against a wall, a tree or some other upright structure, hardy kiwis will twine upward all summer. They can also be grown in containers.

Hardy kiwi vines can grow uncontrollably. Don't be afraid to prune them back if they get out of hand.

Recommended

There are two hardy kiwi vines commonly grown in New England gardens. *A. arguta* (hardy kiwi, bower actinidia) has dark green, heart-shaped leaves, white flowers and smooth-skinned, greenish yellow, edible fruit. *A. kolomikta* (variegated kiwi vine, kolomikta actinidia) has green leaves strongly variegated with pink and white, white flowers and smooth-skinned, greenish yellow, edible fruit.

Both a male and a female vine must be present for fruit to be produced. The plants are often sold in pairs.

Features: white early-summer flowers; edible fruit; twining habit **Height:** 15–30' to indefinite **Spread:** 15–30' to indefinite **Hardiness:** zones 3–8

Honeysuckle
Lonicera

Honeysuckles can be rampant twining vines, but with careful consideration and placement they won't overrun your garden. The fragrance of the flowers makes any effort worthwhile.

Growing

Honeysuckles grow well in **full sun** or **partial shade**. The soil should be **average to fertile, humus rich, moist** and **well drained**.

Tips

Honeysuckle can be trained to grow up a trellis, fence, arbor or other structure. In a large container near a porch it will ramble over the edges of the pot and up the railings with reckless abandon.

Recommended

There are dozens of honeysuckle species, hybrids and cultivars. Check with your local garden center to see what is available. The following are two popular species.

L. caprifolium (Italian honeysuckle, Italian woodbine) bears fragrant, creamy white or yellow flowers in late spring and early summer.

L. sempervirens (trumpet honeysuckle, coral honeysuckle) bears orange or red flowers in late spring and early summer. Many cultivars and hybrids are available with flowers in yellow, red or scarlet,

L. sempervirens (above)
L. x brownii 'Dropmore Scarlet' (below)

including **L. x brownii 'Dropmore Scarlet,'** one of the hardiest of the climbing honeysuckles. It is cold hardy to zone 4 and bears bright red flowers for most of summer.

Features: white, yellow, red late-spring and early-summer flowers; twining habit; fruit
Height: 6–20' **Spread:** 6–20'
Hardiness: zones 5–8

Hops
Humulus

H. lupulus (above & below)

*O*f you sit nearby for an afternoon, you might actually be able to see your hops grow.

Growing

Hops grow best in **full sun**. The soil should be **average to fertile, humus rich, moist** and **well drained**, though established plants adapt to most conditions as long as they are well watered for the first few years.

Tips

Hops will quickly twine around any sturdy support to create a screen or shade a patio or deck. Provide a pergola, arbor, porch rail or even a telephone pole for hops to grow up. Most trellises are too delicate for this vigorous grower.

Recommended

H. lupulus is a fast-growing, twining vine with rough-textured, bright green leaves and stems. The fragrant, cone-like flowers, which are used to flavor beer, are produced only on the female plants and mature from green to beige. A cultivar with golden yellow foliage is also available.

Hops are true perennials; each year the plant sends up shoots from ground level. The previous year's growth will need to be cleared away.

Features: twining habit; dense growth; cone-like, late-summer flowers
Height: 10–20' or more **Spread:** 10–20' or more **Hardiness:** zones 3–8

Japanese Hydrangea Vine

Schizophragma

his vine is similar in appearance to climbing hydrangea but has a few interesting cultivars to add variety.

Growing

Japanese hydrangea vine grows well in **full sun** or **partial shade**. The soil should be **average to fertile, humus rich, moist** and **well drained**.

This vine will have trouble clinging to a smooth-surfaced wall. Attach a few supports to the wall and tie the vines to these. The dense growth will eventually hide the support.

Tips

This vine will cling to any rough surface and looks attractive climbing a wall, fence, tree, pergola or arbor. It also can be used as a groundcover on a bank or allowed to grow up or over a rock wall.

Recommended

S. hydrangeoides is an attractive climbing vine similar in appearance to climbing hydrangea. It bears lacy clusters of white flowers in mid-summer. **'Moonlight'** has silvery blue foliage. **'Roseum'** bears clusters of pink flowers.

This elegant vine adds a touch of glamour to even the most ordinary-looking home.

S. hydrangeoides (above & below)

Features: clinging habit; dark green or silvery foliage; white or pink flowers **Height:** up to 40'
Spread: up to 40' **Hardiness:** zones 5–8

Morning Glory
Ipomoea

I. tricolor (above & below)

I. alba, *commonly called moonflower, is a twining climber that bears sweet-scented, white flowers that only open at night. It is similar in size and habit to the two morning glories listed here.*

Brightly colored flowers are produced in abundance, giving even the dullest fence or wall a splash of excitement.

Growing
Morning glory grows best in **full sun**. The soil should be of **poor to average fertility, light** and **well drained**, though these plants adapt to most soil conditions. They twine around narrow objects to climb and must be provided with a trellis or wires if grown against a fence with broad boards, a wall, or another surface they can't wind around. These plants resent having their roots disturbed, so they are best started as seeds and planted where you want them to grow.

Tips
These annual vines can be grown on fences, walls, trees, trellises and arbors. As groundcovers, morning glories will grow over any objects they encounter. They can also be grown in hanging baskets or containers where they will spill over the edges. Plants self-seed easily.

Recommended
I. purpurea is a twining climber that bears trumpet-shaped flowers in shades of purple, blue, pink or white. Cultivars are available.

I. tricolor is a twining climber that bears trumpet-shaped flowers in shades of blue and purple, often with lighter or white centers. Many cultivars are available, including **'Heavenly Blue,'** with white-centered, sky-blue flowers.

Features: fast-growing twining habit; purple, blue, pink, white flowers; foliage
Height: 6–12' **Spread:** 6–12'
Hardiness: tender annual

Passion Flower

Passiflora

Exotic and mesmerizing, passion flowers are sure to attract attention in your garden.

Growing

Passion flower grows well in **full sun** or **partial shade** in a location **sheltered** from wind and cold. The soil should be of **average fertility, moist** and **well drained**.

Tips

Passion flower is a popular addition to mixed containers and creates an unusual focal point near a door or other entryway. Provided with a trellis or other structure, it will climb quickly all summer, though not as much as some of the other annual vines.

P. caerulea (above & below)

Recommended

P. caerulea is a vigorous, woody climber with deeply lobed leaves. It bears unusual purple-banded, purple-white flowers all summer. It can grow up to 30' tall but usually only grows 5–10' over the course of the summer. Hardy to zone 6, it may survive winter in some of the warmer areas of New England.

Compost passion flowers at the end of the season; cut them back and bring them indoors for the winter where they aren't hardy; or leave them in a sheltered location outdoors where they are hardy.

Features: exotic flowers; attractive foliage
Height: 5–10' **Spread:** variable
Hardiness: zones 6–9; often grown as an annual

Silver Lace Vine
Polygonum

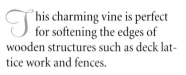

This charming vine is perfect for softening the edges of wooden structures such as deck lattice work and fences.

Growing
Silver lace vine grows well in **full sun, partial shade** or **light shade**. The soil should be of **average to poor fertility, moist** and **well drained**. This plant requires a sturdy support to twine around.

Tips
This vine is useful for creating fast-growing screens, especially on chain-link fences. It can also be trained up an arbor, pergola or trellis.

Recommended
P. aubertii (*Fallopia aubertii*) is a fast-growing, twining, woody climber. The clusters of small, white flowers are produced in late summer and stand out attractively against the heart-shaped leaves. This vigorous grower can overwhelm other vegetation, so make sure you place it where it can grow up a sturdy structure and not over neighboring plants.

P. aubertii (above & below)

Silver lace vine roots where the branches touch the ground, and new plants can sprout from the small pieces of root left in the ground.

Also called: mile-a-minute plant, fleece vine
Features: twining deciduous vine with attractive, white summer flowers; foliage
Height: 25–40' or more   **Spread:** 25–40' or more   **Hardiness:** zones 4–8

Sweet Pea
Lathyrus

Sweet peas are among the most enchanting annuals. Their fragrance is intoxicating, and the flowers in double tones and shimmering shades look like no other annual in the garden.

Growing

Sweet peas prefer **full sun** but tolerate light shade. The soil should be **fertile**, high in **organic matter, moist** and **well drained**. The plants tolerate light frost.

Soak seeds in water for 24 hours or nick them with a nail file before planting them. Planting a second crop of sweet peas about a month after the first one will ensure a longer blooming period. Deadhead all blooms.

Tips

Sweet peas will grow up poles, trellises, fences or over rocks. They cling by wrapping tendrils around whatever they are growing up, so they do best when they have a rough surface, chain-link fence, small twigs or a net to cling to.

Recommended

There are many cultivars of **L. odoratus** available, though many are now small and bushy rather than climbing. **'Bouquet'** is a tall, climbing variety with flowers in a wide range of colors.

L. odoratus cultivars (above & below)

Newer sweet pea cultivars often have less fragrant flowers than old-fashioned cultivars. Look for heritage varieties to enjoy the most fragrant flowers.

Features: clinging habit; fragrant pink, red, purple, lavender, blue, salmon, pale yellow, peach, white, bicolored summer flowers
Height: 1–6' **Spread:** 6–12"
Hardiness: hardy annual

Wisteria

Wisteria

W. sinensis (above & below)

All parts of these plants, including the bean-like pods, are poisonous.

Loose clusters of purple hang like lace from the branches of wisteria. A gardener willing to use garden shears can create beautiful tree forms and attractive arbor specimens.

Growing

Wisterias grow well in **full sun** or **partial shade**. The soil should be of **average fertility, moist** and **well drained**. Vines grown in too fertile a soil will produce a lot of vegetative growth but very few flowers. Avoid planting wisteria near a lawn where fertilizer may leach over to the vine.

Tips

These vines require something to twine around, such as a solidly built arbor or other sturdy structure. You can also train a wisteria to form a small tree. Try to select a permanent site; wisterias don't like being moved. These vigorous vines may send up suckers and can root wherever the branches touch the ground.

Recommended

W. floribunda (Japanese wisteria) bears long, pendulous clusters of fragrant, blue, purple, pink or white flowers in late spring before the leaves emerge. Long, bean-like pods follow.

W. sinensis (Chinese wisteria) bears long, pendant clusters of fragrant, blue-purple flowers in late spring. **'Alba'** has white flowers.

Features: fragrant, blue, purple, pink, white late-spring flowers; foliage; twining habit
Height: 20–50' or more **Spread:** 20–50' or more **Hardiness:** zones 4–9

Canna Lily
Canna

Canna lilies are stunning, dramatic plants that give an exotic flair to any garden.

Growing
Canna lilies grow best in **full sun** in a **sheltered** location. The soil should be **fertile, moist** and **well drained**. Plant out in spring, once soil has warmed. Plants can be started early indoors in containers to get a head start on the growing season. Deadhead to prolong blooming.

Tips
Canna lilies can be grown in a bed or border. They make dramatic specimen plants and can even be included in large planters.

Recommended
A wide range of canna lilies are available, including cultivars and hybrids with green, bronzy, purple or yellow-and-green-striped foliage. Flowers may be white, red, orange, pink, yellow or bicolored. Dwarf cultivars that grow 18–28" tall are also available.

C. 'Red King Humbert' (above & below)

The rhizomes can be lifted after the foliage is killed back in fall. Clean off any clinging dirt, cut off foliage and store them in a cool, frost-free location in slightly moist peat moss. Check on them regularly through winter and if they are starting to sprout, pot them and move them to a bright window until they can be moved outdoors.

Features: decorative foliage; white, red, orange, pink, yellow, bicolored summer flowers **Height:** 18"–6' **Spread:** 12–36" **Hardiness:** zones 7–9; grown as an annual

Crocus

Crocus

C. x vernus cultivars (above & below)

Crocuses are harbingers of spring. They often appear, as if by magic, in full bloom from beneath the melting snow.

Growing

Crocuses grow well in **full sun** or **light, dappled shade**. The soil should be of **poor to average fertility, gritty** and **well drained**. The corms are planted about 4" deep in fall.

Saffron is obtained from the dried, crushed stigmas of C. sativus. *Six plants produce enough spice for one recipe. This fall-blooming plant is hardy to zone 6.*

Tips

Crocuses are almost always planted in groups. Drifts of crocuses can be planted in lawns to provide interest and color while the grass still lies dormant. They can be left to naturalize in beds and borders. Groups of plants will fill in and spread out to provide a bright welcome in spring.

Recommended

Many crocus species, hybrids and cultivars are available. The spring-flowering crocus most people are familiar with is **C. x *vernus***, commonly called Dutch crocus. Many cultivars are available, with flowers in shades of purple, yellow or white, sometimes bicolored or with darker veins.

Features: purple, yellow, white, sometimes bicolored, early-spring flowers **Height:** 2–6"
Spread: 2–4" **Hardiness:** zones 3–8

Daffodil

Narcissus

Many gardeners think of large, yellow, trumpet-shaped flowers when they think of daffodils, but there is plenty of variation in color, form and size among the daffodils.

Growing

Daffodils grow best in **full sun** or **light, dappled shade**. The soil should be **average to fertile, moist** and **well drained**. Bulbs should be planted in fall, 2–8" deep, depending on the size of the bulb. The bigger the bulb the deeper it should be planted. A rule of thumb is to measure the bulb from top to bottom and multiply that number by three to know how deeply to plant.

Tips

Daffodils are often planted where they can be left to naturalize in the light shade beneath a tree or in a woodland garden. In mixed beds and borders, the faded leaves are hidden by the summer foliage of other plants.

Recommended

Many species, hybrids and cultivars of daffodils are available. Flowers come in shades of white, yellow, peach, orange, pink and may also be bicolored. Flowers range from $1^1/_2$–6" across, and can be solitary or borne in clusters. There are about 12 flower form categories.

Features: white, yellow, peach, orange, pink, bicolored spring flowers **Height:** 4–24" **Spread:** 4–12" **Hardiness:** zones 3–9

Dahlia

Dahlia

Dahlia cultivars span a vast array of colors, sizes and flower forms, but breeders have yet to develop true blue, scented or frost-hardy selections.

The variation in size, shape and color of dahlia flowers is astonishing. You are sure to find at least one that appeals to you.

Growing

Dahlias prefer **full sun**. The soil should be **fertile**, rich in **organic matter, moist** and **well drained**. All dahlias are tender, tuberous perennials treated as annuals. Tubers can be purchased and started early indoors. The tubers can also be lifted in fall and stored in a cool, frost-free location over winter. Pot them and keep them in a bright room when they start sprouting in mid- to late winter. Deadhead to keep plants tidy and blooming.

Tips

Dahlias make attractive, colorful additions to a mixed border. The smaller varieties make good edging plants and the larger ones make good alternatives to shrubs. Varieties with unusual or interesting flowers are attractive specimen plants.

Recommended

Of the many dahlia hybrids, most are grown from tubers, but a few can be started from seed. Many hybrids are sold based on flower shape, such as collarette, decorative or peony-flowered. The flowers range in size from 2–12" and are available in shades of purple, pink, white, yellow, orange or red, with some bicolored. Check with your local garden center to see what is available.

Features: purple, pink, white, yellow, orange, red, bicolored summer flowers; attractive foliage; bushy habit **Height:** 8"–5' **Spread:** 8–18" **Hardiness:** tender perennial; treat as an annual

Flowering Onion

Allium

*F*lowering onions, with their striking, ball-like to loose, nodding clusters of flowers, are sure to attract attention.

Growing

Flowering onions grow best in **full sun**. The soil should be **average to fertile, moist** and **well drained**. Plant bulbs in fall, 2–4" deep, depending on size of bulb.

Tips

Flowering onions are best planted in groups in a bed or border where they can be left to naturalize. Most will self-seed when left to their own devices. The foliage, which tends to fade just as the plants come into flower, can be hidden with groundcover or a low, bushy companion plant.

Recommended

Several flowering onion species, hybrids and cultivars have gained popularity for their decorative, pink, purple, white, yellow, blue or maroon flowers. These include **A. aflatunense**, with dense, globe-like clusters of lavender flowers; **A. caeruleum** (blue globe onion), with globe-like clusters of blue flowers; **A. cernuum** (nodding or wild onion), with loose, drooping clusters of pink flowers; and **A. giganteum** (giant onion), a big plant that grows up to 6' tall, with large, globe-shaped clusters of pinky purple flowers.

A. giganteum (above), *A. cernuum* (below)

Although the leaves have an onion scent when bruised, the flowers are often sweetly fragrant. They make a great addition to dried-flower arrangements.

Features: pink, purple, white, yellow, blue, maroon summer flowers; cylindrical or strap-shaped leaves Height: 1–6'
Spread: 2–12" Hardiness: zones 3–9

Lily
Lilium

L. Asiatic Hybrids (above)
L. Oriental Hybrids 'Stargazer' (below)

Decorative clusters of large, richly colored blooms grace these tall plants. Flowers are produced at differing times of the season, depending on the hybrid, so it is possible to have lilies blooming all season if a variety of cultivars are chosen.

Growing

Lilies grow best in **full sun** but like to have their **roots shaded**. The soil should be rich in **organic matter, fertile, moist** and **well drained**.

Tips

Lilies are often grouped in beds and borders and can be naturalized in woodland gardens and near water features. These plants are narrow but tall; plant at least three plants together to create some volume.

Recommended

The many species, hybrids and cultivars available are grouped by type. Visit your local garden center to see what is available. The following are two popular groups of lilies.
Asiatic Hybrids bear clusters of flowers in early or mid-summer and are available in a wide range of colors.
Oriental Hybrids bear clusters of large, fragrant flowers in mid- and late summer. Colors are usually white, pink or red. (Zones 5–7)

Lily bulbs should be planted in fall before the first frost but can also be planted in spring if bulbs are available.

Features: early, mid- or late-season flowers in shades of orange, yellow, peach, pink, purple, red, white **Height:** 2–5' **Spread:** 12" **Hardiness:** zones 4–7

Scilla

Scilla

These easy-to-grow spring bloomers look wonderful in mass plantings and are resistant to browsing by deer.

Growing

Scilla grows well in **full sun, partial shade** or **light shade**. The soil should be **average to fertile, humus rich** and **well drained**. Bulbs should be planted 3–4" deep in fall.

Tips

Scilla makes a lovely addition to mixed beds and borders where the bulbs can be interplanted among other plants. They can also be planted in lawns, meadow gardens and woodland gardens where they can be left to naturalize.

Recommended

S. bifolia is a low-growing plant with narrow strap-shaped leaves. It bears clusters of blue or purple flowers in spring. It grows 4–6" tall and spreads about 3".

S. scilloides (Chinese scilla) also has narrow strap-shaped leaves and bears large clusters of small, purple-pink flowers in late summer and fall. It grows 6–8" tall and spreads about 4". (Zones 4–8)

S. siberica (Siberian squill, spring squill) has wider strap-shaped leaves than the other two species. It bears small clusters of bright blue, nodding flowers in spring. It grows 4–8" tall and spreads about 2". Cultivars are available. (Zones 5–8)

S. *siberica* (above & below)

These plants can self-seed prolifically. Keep your eyes open for the small, grass-like seedlings so you can avoid pulling them up if you want more plants, or pull them up if you don't.

Also called: squill **Features:** blue, purple spring or fall flowers **Height:** 4–8" **Spread:** 2–4" **Hardiness:** zones 3–8

Tulip

Tulipa

T. hybrids (above & below)

Tulips, with their beautiful, often garishly colored flowers, are a welcome sight as we enjoy the warm days of spring.

Growing

Tulips grow best in **full sun**. In light or partial shade the flowers tend to bend toward the light. The soil should be **fertile** and **well drained**. Plant bulbs in fall, 4–6" deep, depending on size of bulb. Bulbs that have been cold treated can be planted in spring. Although tulips can

During the tulipomania of the 1630s, the bulbs were worth many times their weight in gold, and many tulip speculators lost massive fortunes when the mania ended.

repeat bloom, many hybrids perform best if planted new each year.

Tips

Tulips provide the best display when mass planted or planted in groups in flowerbeds and borders. They can also be grown in containers and can be forced to bloom early in pots indoors. Some of the species and older cultivars can be naturalized in meadow and wildflower gardens.

Recommended

There are about 100 species of tulips and thousands of hybrids and cultivars. They are generally divided into 15 groups based on bloom time and flower appearance. They come in dozens of shades, with many bicolored or multi-colored varieties. Blue is the only shade not available. Check with your local garden center in early fall for the best selection.

Features: spring flowers **Height:** 6–30"
Spread: 2–8" **Hardiness:** zones 3–8;
sometimes treated as an annual

Winter Aconite
Eranthis

E. hyemalis (above & below)

One of the earliest plants to bloom, the carpet of yellow flowers is a welcome sight, signaling winter's end and the approach of spring.

Growing

Winter aconite grows well in **full sun** or **light shade**. The soil should be **fertile, humus rich, moist** and **well drained**. Plants go dormant during summer, but the soil should still be kept moist. Plant tubers about 3" deep.

Tips

Winter aconite is a good plant for naturalizing in moist, lightly shaded areas under trees and shrubs. It can also be used around water features.

Recommended

E. hyemalis is a low, spreading plant. The whorls of leaves form a bright green ruff around the base of the yellow flowers. Plants spread quickly to form large colonies.

The plant sap can cause skin irritation and upset stomach if ingested. Wear gloves or wash your hands thoroughly after handling.

Features: bright yellow early-spring flowers; glossy green foliage
Height: 2–4" **Spread:** 24" to indefinite **Hardiness:** zones 4–5

Basil
Ocimum

The sweet, fragrant leaves of fresh basil add a delicious, licorice-like flavor to salads and tomato-based dishes.

Growing
Basil grows best in a **warm, sheltered** location in **full sun**. The soil should be **fertile, moist** and **well drained**. Pinch tips regularly to encourage bushy growth. Plant out or direct sow seed after frost danger has passed in spring.

Tips
Although basil will grow best in a warm spot outdoors, it can be grown successfully in a pot by a bright window indoors to provide you with fresh leaves all year.

Recommended
O. basilicum is one of the most popular of the culinary herbs. There are dozens of varieties, including ones with large or tiny, green or purple and smooth or ruffled leaves.

O. basilicum 'Genovese' and 'Cinnamon' (above)
O. basilicum 'Genovese' (below)

Basil is a good companion plant for tomatoes—both like warm, moist growing conditions, and when you pick tomatoes for a salad you'll also remember to include a few sprigs of basil.

Features: fragrant, decorative leaves
Height: 12–24" **Spread:** 12–18"
Hardiness: tender annual

Chives

Allium

The delicate onion flavor of chives is best enjoyed fresh. Mix chives into dips or sprinkle them on salads and baked potatoes.

Growing

Chives grow best in **full sun**. The soil should be **fertile, moist** and **well drained**, but chives adapt to most soil conditions. These plants are easy to start from seed, but they do like the soil temperature to stay above 65° F before they will germinate, so seeds started directly in the garden are unlikely to sprout before early summer.

Tips

Chives are decorative enough to be included in a mixed or herbaceous border and can be left to naturalize. In an herb garden, chives should be given plenty of space to allow self-seeding.

Recommended

A. schoenoprasum forms a clump of bright green, cylindrical leaves. Clusters of pinky purple flowers are produced in early and midsummer. Varieties with white or pink flowers are also available.

Chives will spread with reckless abandon as the clumps grow larger and the plants self-seed.

A. schoenoprasum (above & below)

Chives are said to increase appetite and encourage good digestion.

Features: foliage; form; white, pink, pinky purple flowers **Height:** 8–24" **Spread:** 12" or more **Hardiness:** zones 3–9

Coriander • Cilantro
Coriandrum

C oriander is a multi-purpose herb. The leaves, called cilantro and used in salads, salsas and soups, and the seeds, called coriander and used in pies, chutneys and marmalades, have distinct flavors and culinary uses.

Growing
Coriander prefers **full sun** but tolerates partial shade. The soil should be **fertile, light** and **well drained**. These plants dislike humid conditions and do best during a dry summer.

Tips
Coriander has pungent leaves and is best planted where people will not have to brush past it. It is, however, a delight to behold when in flower. Add a plant or two here and there throughout your borders and vegetable garden, both for the visual appeal and to attract beneficial insects.

Recommended
C. sativum forms a clump of lacy basal foliage above which large, loose clusters of tiny, white flowers are produced. The seeds ripen in late summer and fall.

The delicate, cloud-like clusters of flowers attract pollinating insects such as butterflies and bees, as well as abundant predatory insects that help keep pest insects to a minimum.

C. sativum (above & below)

Features: form; foliage; white flowers; seeds **Height:** 18–24" **Spread:** 8–18"
Hardiness: tender annual

Dill
Anethum

Dill leaves and seeds are probably best known for their use as pickling herbs, though they have a wide variety of other culinary uses.

Growing

Dill grows best in **full sun** in a **sheltered** location out of strong winds. The soil should be of **poor to average fertility, moist** and **well drained**. Sow seeds every couple of weeks in spring and early summer to ensure a regular supply of leaves. Plants should not be grown near fennel because they will cross-pollinate and the seeds of both plants will lose their distinct flavors.

Tips

With its feathery leaves, dill is an attractive addition to a mixed bed or border. It can be included in a vegetable garden but does well in any sunny location. It also attracts predatory insects to the garden.

Recommended

A. graveolens forms a clump of feathery foliage. Clusters of yellow flowers are borne at the tops of sturdy stems.

Dill turns up frequently in historical records as both a culinary and medicinal herb. It was used by the Egyptians and Romans and is mentioned in the Bible.

A. graveolens (above & below)

A popular Scandinavian dish called gravalax is made by marinating a fillet of salmon with the leaves and seeds of dill.

Features: feathery, edible foliage; yellow summer flowers; edible seeds **Height:** 2–5'
Spread: 12" or more **Hardiness:** annual

Lavender

Lavandula

L. angustifolia (above & below)

With both aromatic and ornamental qualities, lavender is considered the queen of herbs.

Growing

Lavenders grow best in **full sun**. The soil should be **average to fertile, alkaline** and **well drained**. Once established, these plants are heat and drought tolerant. Protect plants from winter cold and wind by placing them in a sheltered spot and mulching them in fall. Plants can be sheared in spring or after flowering.

Tips

Lavenders are wonderful, aromatic edging plants. They can be planted in drifts or as specimens in small spaces, and can be used to form low hedges.

Recommended

L. angustifolia (English lavender) is a bushy, aromatic plant. It grows about 24" tall, with an equal spread. It bears spikes of light purple flowers from midsummer to fall. The many cultivars include plants with white or pink flowers, silvery gray to olive green foliage and dwarf or compact habits.

L. x *intermedia* (lavandin) is a natural hybrid between English lavender and spike lavender (*L. latifolia*). It grows about 36" tall, with an equal spread. The flowers are held on long spikes. Cultivars are available.

Features: purple, pink, blue, white mid-summer to fall flowers; fragrance; evergreen foliage; habit **Height:** 8–36" **Spread:** up to 4'
Hardiness: zones 5–9

Mint
Mentha

The cool, refreshing flavor of mint lends itself to tea and other hot or cold beverages. Mint sauce, made from freshly chopped leaves, is often served with lamb.

Growing
Mint grows well in **full sun** or **partial shade**. The soil should be **average to fertile, humus rich** and **moist**. These plants spread vigorously by rhizomes and may need a barrier in the soil to restrict their spread.

Tips
Mint is a good ground-cover for damp spots. It grows well along ditches that may only be periodically wet. It also can be used in beds and borders but may overwhelm less vigorous plants.

The flowers attract bees, butterflies and other pollinators to the garden.

Recommended
There are many species, hybrids and cultivars of mint. **Spearmint** (*M. spicata*), **peppermint** (*M.* x *piperita*) and **orange mint** (*M.* x *piperita citrata*) are three of the most commonly grown culinary varieties. There are also more decorative varieties with variegated or curly leaves as well as varieties with unusual, fruit-scented leaves.

M. x *piperita* 'Chocolate' (above)
M. x *gracilis* (decorative variety; below)

A few sprigs of fresh mint added to a pitcher of iced tea gives it an extra zip.

Features: fragrant foliage; purple, pink, white summer flowers **Height:** 6–36"
Spread: 36" or more **Hardiness:** zones 4–8

Oregano • Marjoram
Origanum

Oregano and marjoram are two of the best known and most frequently used herbs. They are popular in stuffings, soups and stews, and no pizza is complete until it has been sprinkled with fresh or dried oregano leaves.

Growing

Oregano and marjoram grow best in **full sun**. The soil should be of **poor to average fertility, neutral to alkaline** and **well drained**. The flowers attract pollinators to the garden.

Tips

These bushy perennials make a lovely addition to any border and can be trimmed to form low hedges.

O. vulgare 'Polyphant' (above)
O. vulgare 'Aureum' (below)

In Greek, oros means 'mountain' and ganos means 'joy,' so oregano translates as 'joy of the mountain.'

Recommended

O. majorana (marjoram) is upright and shrubby, with light green, hairy leaves. It bears white or pink flowers in summer and can be grown as an annual where it is not hardy.

O. vulgare var. **hirtum** (oregano, Greek oregano) is the most flavorful culinary variety of oregano. The low, bushy plant has hairy, gray-green leaves and bears white flowers. Many other interesting varieties of *O. vulgare* are available, including those with golden, variegated or curly leaves.

Features: fragrant foliage; white or pink summer flowers; bushy habit **Height:** 12–32"
Spread: 8–18" **Hardiness:** zones 5–9

Parsley
Petroselinum

P. crispum (above), *P. crispum* var. *crispum* (below)

Although usually used as a garnish, parsley is rich in vitamins and minerals and is reputed to freshen the breath after garlic- or onion-rich foods are eaten.

Growing

Parsley grows well in **full sun** or **partial shade**. The soil should be of **average to rich fertility, humus rich, moist** and **well drained**. Direct sow seeds because the plants resent transplanting. If you start seeds early, use peat pots so the plants can be potted or planted out without disruption.

Tips

Containers of parsley can be kept close to the house for easy picking. The bright green leaves and compact growth habit make parsley a good edging plant for beds and borders.

Features: attractive foliage **Height:** 8–24"
Spread: 12–24" **Hardiness:** zones 5–8;
grown as an annual

Recommended

P. crispum forms a clump of bright green, divided leaves. This plant is biennial but is usually grown as an annual because it is the leaves that are desired and not the flowers or seeds. Cultivars may have flat or curly leaves. Flat leaves are more flavorful and curly are more decorative. Dwarf cultivars are also available.

Parsley leaves make a tasty and nutritious addition to salads. Tear freshly picked leaves and sprinkle them over your mixed greens.

Rosemary
Rosmarinus

R. officinalis (above & below)

To overwinter a container-grown plant, keep it in light or partial shade outdoors in summer, then put it in a sunny window indoors for winter and keep it well watered, but allow it to dry out slightly between waterings.

The needle-like leaves of rosemary are used to flavor a wide variety of culinary dishes, including chicken, pork, lamb, rice, tomato and egg dishes.

Growing
Rosemary prefers **full sun** but tolerates partial shade. The soil should be of **poor to average fertility** and **well drained**. These tender shrubs must be moved indoors for the winter.

Tips
Rosemary is often grown in a shrub border where hardy. Here, where it is not hardy, it is usually grown in a container as a specimen or with other plants. Low-growing, spreading plants can be included in a rock garden, or can be grown along the top of a retaining wall and in hanging baskets.

Recommended
R. officinalis is a dense, bushy evergreen shrub with narrow, dark green leaves. The habit varies somewhat between cultivars, from strongly upright to prostrate and spreading. Flowers are usually in shades of blue, but pink-flowered cultivars are available. Cultivars are available that can survive in zone 6 in a sheltered location with winter protection. Plants rarely reach their mature size when grown in containers.

Features: fragrant evergreen foliage; bright blue, sometimes pink, summer flowers
Height: 8"–4' **Spread:** 1–4'
Hardiness: zones 8–10

Sage
Salvia

Sage is perhaps best known as a flavoring for stuffing, but it has a great range of uses, including in soups, stews, sausages and dumplings.

Growing

Sage prefers **full sun** but tolerates light shade. The soil should be of **average fertility** and **well drained**. These plants benefit from a light mulch of compost each year. They are drought tolerant once established.

Tips

Sage is an attractive plant for borders; it can be used to add volume to the middle, as an edging or as a feature plant near the front. Sage can also be grown in mixed planters.

S. officinalis 'Icterina' (above), *S. officinalis* 'Purpurea' (below)

Recommended

S. officinalis is a woody, mounding plant with soft gray-green leaves. Spikes of light purple flowers appear in early and mid-summer. Many cultivars with attractive foliage are available, including the silver-leaved **'Berggarten,'** the yellow-margined **'Icterina,'** the purple-leaved **'Purpurea,'** and the purple, green and cream variegated **'Tricolor,'** which has a pink flush to the new growth.

Sage has been used since at least ancient Greek times as a medicinal and culinary herb, and it continues to be widely used for both these purposes today.

Features: fragrant, decorative foliage; blue or purple summer flowers **Height:** 12–24"
Spread: 18–36" **Hardiness:** zones 5–8

Thyme
Thymus

T. vulgaris (above), *T. x citriodorus* (below)

Thyme is a popular culinary herb used in soups, stews, casseroles and with roasts.

Growing

Thyme prefers **full sun**. The soil should be **neutral to alkaline** and of **poor to average fertility**. **Good drainage** is essential. It is beneficial to work leaf mold and sharp limestone gravel into the soil to improve structure and drainage.

Tips

Thyme is useful for sunny, dry locations at the front of borders, between or beside paving stones, on rock walls and in rock gardens and containers.

Once the plants have finished flowering, shear them back by about half to encourage new growth and to prevent the plants from becoming too woody.

Recommended

T. x citriodorus (lemon-scented thyme) forms a mound of lemon-scented, dark green foliage. The flowers are pale pink. Cultivars with silver- or gold-margined leaves are available.

T. vulgaris (common thyme) forms a bushy mound of dark green leaves. The flowers may be purple, pink or white. Cultivars with variegated leaves are available.

These plants are bee magnets when blooming; thyme honey is pleasantly herbal and goes very well with biscuits.

Features: bushy habit; fragrant, decorative foliage; purple, pink, white flowers
Height: 8–16" **Spread:** 8–16"
Hardiness: zones 4–9

Glossary

Acid soil: soil with a pH lower than 7.0

Annual: a plant that germinates, flowers, sets seed and dies in one growing season

Alkaline soil: soil with a pH higher than 7.0

Basal leaves: leaves that form from the crown, at the base of the plant

Bract: a modified leaf at the base of a flower or flower cluster

Corm: a bulb-like, food-storing, underground stem, resembling a bulb without scales

Crown: the part of the plant at or just below soil level where the shoots join the roots

Cultivar: a cultivated plant variety with one or more distinct differences from the species, e.g., in flower color or disease resistance

Damping off: fungal disease causing seedlings to rot at soil level and topple over

Deadhead: to remove spent flowers to maintain a neat appearance and encourage a longer blooming season

Direct sow: to sow seeds directly in the garden

Dormancy: a period of plant inactivity, usually during winter or unfavorable conditions

Double flower: a flower with an unusually large number of petals

Genus: a category of biological classification between the species and family levels; the first word in a scientific name indicates the genus

Grafting: a type of propagation in which a stem or bud of one plant is joined onto the rootstock of another plant of a closely related species

Hardy: capable of surviving unfavorable conditions, such as cold weather or frost, without protection

Hip: the fruit of a rose, containing the seeds

Humus: decomposed or decomposing organic material in the soil

Hybrid: a plant resulting from natural or human-induced cross-breeding between varieties, species or genera

Inflorescence: a flower cluster

Male clone: a plant that may or may not produce pollen but that will not produce fruit, seed or seedpods

Neutral soil: soil with a pH of 7.0

Perennial: a plant that takes three or more years to complete its life cycle

pH: a measure of acidity or alkalinity; the soil pH influences availability of nutrients for plants

Rhizome: a root-like, food-storing stem that grows horizontally at or just below soil level, from which new shoots may emerge

Rootball: the root mass and surrounding soil of a plant

Seedhead: dried, inedible fruit that contains seeds; the fruiting stage of the inflorescence

Self-seeding: reproducing by means of seeds without human assistance, so that new plants constantly replace those that die

Semi-double flower: a flower with petals in two or three rings

Single flower: a flower with a single ring of typically four or five petals

Species: the fundamental unit of biological classification; the entity from which cultivars and varieties are derived

Standard: a shrub or small tree grown with an erect main stem, accomplished either through pruning and training or by grafting the plant onto a tall, straight stock

Sucker: a shoot that comes up from the root, often some distance from the plant; it can be separated to form a new plant once it develops its own roots

Tender: incapable of surviving the climatic conditions of a given region and requiring protection from frost or cold

Tuber: the thick section of a rhizome bearing nodes and buds

Variegation: foliage that has more than one color, often patched or striped or bearing leaf margins of a different color

Variety: a naturally occurring variant of a species

Index of Recommended Species Plant Names

Bold indicates main entries; *italics* indicates botanical names.

Author Biographies

Thomas Mickey has been gardening in New England for 25 years. He is a landscape designer who will graduate next year from Harvard University's Landscape Institute. His garden is in Rye, NH, which is near the seacoast. He writes a regular garden column for *Seacoast Media* in Portsmouth, NH and the *Brockton Enterprise* in Brockton, MA. He has written two books and published several articles in his role as Professor of Communication Studies at Bridgewater State College in Bridgewater, MA.

Alison Beck has gardened since she was a child. She has a diploma in horticulture and a degree in creative writing. Alison has co-authored many best-selling gardening guides. Her books showcase her talent for practical advice and her passion for gardening.